THE

DONUT

KING

THE

THE RAGS TO RICHES STORY

DONUT

OF A POOR IMMIGRANT

KING

WHO CHANGED THE WORLD

TED NGOY

The Donut King

Published by
Ted Ngoy

ISBN: 978-0-9994326-0-0
eISBN: 978-0-9994326-1-7

Cover and Interior Design: GKS Creative

Dedicated to my dearest mother, Taing Cheng,
whose strength and spirit uplift me still,
and to Christy (Suganthini), whose love
and unfailing grace saved my life.

PART I
OF VI

BEFORE I TOUCHED DOWN ON THE GOLDEN COAST OF CALIFORNIA without a cent to my name, before I made and lost millions of dollars, only to make it all back, and before evil thugs destroyed my beautiful homeland and killed my people, there was a girl who smelled of flowers. We were classmates in the French high school in Phnom Penh, the capital of Cambodia. I sat right behind Suganthini, close enough to reach out and graze her long, dark hair. But the proximity was an illusion. She was the daughter of an aristocratic family, one of the richest and most powerful in Cambodia. Her beauty and her status made her the sole object of admiration for most of the boys at our school. They bought her gifts and wrote poems proclaiming their love. I, on the other hand, was the son of a poor Chinese woman who had immigrated to Cambodia years earlier. My father left us, and I grew up with my mother and sisters in a rural town called Sisophon in the northwest corner of the country. I was a mediocre student, and I was shy and quiet. We were worlds apart.

Still, I knew I was in love. And I knew something else, a secret that has brought me great wealth and incredible pain. From a young age, I understood that being the long shot—the man who has nothing and therefore nothing to lose—can be an advantage. When you are the long shot, you allow yourself to take chances. And success in life favors those who take chances.

The fact that I was studying at Voltaire High School in the capital was something of a miracle. The school was expensive, and though my small shared apartment in the hottest room of a walkup building was cheap by Phnom Penh standards, it was a terrible burden for my mother.

I grew up in Sisophon, a dusty town thirty miles from the border between Cambodia and Thailand. There were few cars at the time, and the motorbikes that choke the roads today were still rare. Locals used bicycles to travel to and from the rice plantations where most of the townspeople lived, and there wasn't much in the way of commerce or entertainment. It was a poor place, but it was also peaceful, with the slow, pleasant rhythms of a rural backwater. Later, when everything became frenzied and dangerous, I would remember that peaceful time fondly.

When I was a child, my mother, sisters, and I lived in an old wooden house by the roadside. It was a point of pride for our family. We were poor, and my mother was Chinese, so we were looked down upon by some. But we had more than the very poorest people who lived on the outskirts of town, closer to the rice fields, and that was a point of great pride. The four of us shared a single wooden room where we slept and cooked and ate our meals. My mother carried the legacy of a Cantonese upbringing when she moved to Cambodia with my father, and her meals were always served warm and ushered to the table gingerly, like small gifts to her children. My mother and father met while my father was studying in China, and my mother was hopeful about her new life when she decided to leave her homeland and follow him to Cambodia, but when my sisters and I were still young, our father fled to Thailand. My mother didn't speak Khmer, the Cambodian language, and was left to raise us alone.

With no education or capital, my mother had few options for making money. She earned a meager income traveling to Thailand to buy and sell goods, which she traded for a small profit. It was no easy feat. The train to the Thai border left at 5:00 in the morning, which meant my mother had to set out well before daylight. She lugged thirty kilograms of chicken, pork, beef, or vegetables that she bought or borrowed from neighbors the day before. When she arrived, she traded what she had and looked for products she knew she could sell back home. Though she had little education and only spoke Chinese, she was a smart trader and usually managed to come out on top. My mother's best-selling product was alcohol, especially Johnny Walker, which was much cheaper to buy in Cambodia. But it was illegal to bring bottles of alcohol across the border into Thailand without paying a customs tax, the additional cost of which erased my mother's profit. That meant she had to smuggle the bottles on the train.

The customs officers were vigilant, sometimes merciless. They searched passengers and remembered the faces of past offenders, and from time to time they beat up smugglers or threw them in jail. My mother went to great lengths to keep from being caught, hanging off the back of railcars or squatting on the platform between cars to stay hidden. It was a dangerous way to make money. Twice she fell from the moving train and sustained serious injuries.

Both times, farmers passing in buffalo carts picked her up and brought her to the hospital, where I remember visiting her. I wasn't older than seven or eight, and but I can still feel the shock of seeing her covered in blood, looking small. I remember the anger, as well. The engineers had left her on the tracks to die while the train charged on. The lives of the poor were not valued then, and if we are looking for the seeds of the genocide that would change the lives of every Cambodian, they are easy to spot in the ability of good people to ignore suffering.

As a young boy, I was left alone during the day while my mother traveled to the border. I had the habit of running around with no pants on as a five-year-old, a story our neighbors refused to let me forget as I grew older. Though I spoke Chinese at home, Khmer came easily to me. There were plenty of kids around, and I fancied myself a neighborhood leader. We played games of tag and put on childish theater shows. I organized a thriving food exchange, asking children to bring vegetables or cans from their parents' gardens or cupboards, which we traded among ourselves. Every afternoon at one o'clock, I enlisted a few friends to walk the three miles to the train station, where my mother would soon disembark with the products she'd traded for—soap, spices, sugar, clothes, and silk. Cambodia was an agricultural country and produced almost no finished products. My friends and I would help carry her haul back to the house, and she rewarded us with delicious food.

•••

Chinese immigrants go to great lengths to ensure their children receive an education. When I was old enough, my mother sent me to a local Chinese primary school. There were so few Chinese families in Sisophon that the school could only support four grades instead of six. When I finished fourth grade, I assumed my school days were behind me. But my mother had other plans. I was to travel to the provincial capital, Battambang, which was about forty-five miles away, to finish fifth and sixth grade. The idea of leaving home frightened me, and I begged my mother to let me stay with her. In her quiet way, she responded that the decision had been made.

One morning, skipping her usual trip to the border, she walked me to the bus station. I carried a small bundle of clothes, and I cried. When the bus arrived, she gave the driver some instructions. Then she waved goodbye and told me she'd see me at the next holiday. I passed the bumpy ride in fear. At least I would know one familiar face in Battambang. One of the teachers from my Chinese primary school had secured a job and was transferring that year, and he had always been very nice to me.

When we arrived in Battambang, I climbed off the bus with my bundle of clothes in my hands and looked around. Battambang wasn't a big city, but compared to Sisophon it seemed like the center of the universe. Everything was bigger, faster, and scarier. Swarms of people passed on bicycles. To my horror, I realized my teacher, who was supposed to meet me at the bus stop, was nowhere to be seen. Breathing heavily, I sat down on a bench and waited for two hours. When he showed up, I ran to him and clung to his leg.

Without my friends or my mother, whom I loved and relied on in ways I didn't yet understand, I felt lost at the new school. There was no telephone, and letters took days to arrive. The classes were much bigger than I was used to, with forty students crammed into a room. Life in the dormitory was highly regimented, and I longed for endless afternoons playing with friends. Every morning when we woke, we ate porridge with an egg. After that we attended class. Then lunch and more classes. After dinner, we met with teachers to review schoolwork.

Typically, families sent boys off to boarding school with pocket money to buy supplies or extra food. Mostly the money went to small luxuries instead of necessary supplies. After dinner, some of the boys in the school liked to go to a market nearby to buy ice cream. My mother had given me 1,000 riel for the term. It wasn't much, but it was more than she could comfortably afford. I vowed not to spend the money unless I absolutely had to, which hurt me socially. But it was worth it. At the end of the first term, I returned home and put 500 riel in front of her. She was happy just to have me back for a short time, but I know she appreciated the money.

Just as I had enlisted the neighborhood kids to help clean our house, being able to give something to make my mother's life easier made me proud. My motivation for making money has always been to provide for loved ones and community. It's not selflessness—I suspect I get more out of the bargain than anyone else. In this case, the look on my mother's face when I put her money on the table was easily worth a semester of ice cream.

Battambang humbled me. I was like a boy king in our tiny village, but in Battambang I was neither the smartest nor the most popular student. While other boys had cousins or uncles visit on weekends, I had no one. The teachers looked after me, and I especially remember the kindness of the headmaster, who knew I had grown up without a father. But it was a lonely life, confined largely to classrooms and the dormitory. When I graduated, I went on to high school. My time there was equally lonely, and I looked forward to the break we got every six months, when I could travel home and see my mother.

I did find some solace in basketball. I threw myself at the sport. For a few hours before and after school, I stepped onto the court and felt that old feeling of being in charge. It was an unusual experience: in the classroom I was invisible, but on the court, with the ball in my hand, I was often the best player. As an attacking guard, I zipped around looking for opportunities to score. At the time, most players shot in a clumsy two-handed style, but I was a natural right-handed shooter, and I was accurate. I was also short, even by Cambodian standards. I made up for it with speed, and I typically scored the most points for my team during games. One of my coaches pointed out that many of my scoring opportunities came after I stole a ball on defense.

There is something about creating opportunities while on the retreat that has always appealed to me, and it is a theme that would recur again and again in my wild life. I was good enough at basketball to be chosen to represent Battambang in a national youth league. It was a high honor, and if I still wasn't the most popular student at school, my skill on the court at least earned me some respect.

...

Battambang had no high school, so again I had to travel far from home. Scrimping and saving, my mother sent me to Phnom Penh, the capital of Cambodia, for high school. My time there was unremarkable and mostly confined to the dormitory—I didn't explore the city at all, too scared to venture out on my own. When I graduated, I had to confront an uncomfortable truth: I had no idea what I wanted to do with my life. Unlike in the United States, where betterment and prosperity are usually the goals and young adults go to college before choosing their careers, Cambodia still operated under an unofficial caste system. The children of elites and the wellborn were destined to become the administrative and ruling class, while a large spectrum of merchants, bankers, traders, and farmers filled out the lower rungs of society, each in his precise place.

The caste system was partly cultural, but it was reinforced and solidified under French rule. From 1887 to 1954, Cambodia was part of French Indochina, a grouping of French colonial territories in Southeast Asia that included portions of Vietnam and Laos. Cambodian leaders nominally ran the country, but Paris was firmly in charge.

Life under French rule saw some improvements for Cambodia, but without self-determination, the country seethed with discontent. For France, Cambodia was little more than a buffer between the Kingdom of Siam, now known as Thailand, and the more economically important territory of Vietnam, which also belonged to France. To break even in Cambodia, the French levied large taxes on citizens, which kept people poor and disgruntled. France did bring wonderful new cultural elements and an influx of modern conveniences, like electronic appliances and automobiles, but the cost to the country's morale was high.

Following World War II, France's capacity to administer its colonial empire was greatly diminished. Meanwhile, the region was quickly becoming the first major battleground in a looming confrontation between capitalism and communism. Communist movements in Vietnam, Cambodia's eastern neighbor, resulted in the first Indochina War in the mid-1940s, as Hồ Chí Minh's Việt Minh guerrilla forces fought the French Union's Expeditionary Corps. The world's superpowers met in Geneva in 1954 in hopes of putting an end to rising tensions. Because of that meeting, Vietnam was split into northern and southern zones, while Cambodia and Laos, our northern neighbor, were granted independence. Leading up to the first elections, Cambodia's king, Norodom Sihanouk, abdicated his throne to run for office, choosing to call himself "Prince."

Prince Sihanouk won the election and restored much-needed pride to Cambodia, which for generations had been victimized by Thailand and Vietnam and neutered by French rule. It was in this first blush of independence that I completed my primary and secondary schooling and returned home to my mother's house in Sisophon. In generations past, I might have stayed on to become a merchant, building on the skills my mother had mastered after decades of daily excursions to the Thai border. But in a decade of new opportunity, I grew bored and restless after a few months at home. My mother saw how impatient and uninspired the time at home made me, so like any good Chinese mother, she encouraged me to continue my education.

There was a well-known French school in Phnom Penh where I could learn French and study English. Both languages represented new worlds, and the idea of living in the capital appealed to me. My mother agreed to pay for the school, which cost more than she could easily afford, and I returned to Phnom Penh. This time, I vowed to get to know my new home city.

After Cambodia gained independence in 1953, Prince Sihanouk began rapid development of Phnom Penh. Though the city had fewer than a half-million people, it quickly became the most advanced in Southeast Asia, the so-called pearl of the region. Architects who studied abroad under French rule came back with support of Prince Sihanouk, and they began transforming the capital one building at a time. New sewage and transportation infrastructure sprouted overnight. Public space became a priority, and the city teemed with lush parks full of vegetation and fountains. New theaters, conference halls, and monuments gave residents an enormous sense of pride, and sporting contests attracted huge crowds to the new Olympic Stadium. The optimism was palpable when I arrived in Phnom Penh in 1957.

There were about 300 students at Voltaire School, and many came from well-to-do families. I took a room on the fourth floor of a walk-up building that came with a hot plate, a couple of chairs, and a hard mat to sleep on. There was no air conditioning back then, and the heat and the long walk upstairs made the top floors of buildings less desirable, and so more affordable. Once I had dropped my bags, I looked out the window to the street below. I was in my country's biggest city, and I was an adult and a high school graduate. Like Cambodia in those heady days, I felt a sense of nascent freedom.

On the first day of class, I walked in and glanced at the other pupils. Most of the students seemed to know one another. Many had grown up together in a wealthy section of the city. As I was taking in my new surroundings and looking for a seat, I noticed a girl at the front of the room. I sat behind her and couldn't take my eyes off the back of her head. I believe I only heard one word the teacher spoke all day—when he called roll, he said the girl's name: Suganthini. I have carried the sweet sound of those letters with me ever since.

•••

If all of Cambodia was welling with pride at our newfound independence, we nonetheless clung to the cultural yardstick the French had beaten us over the head with. The most prized buildings were a stylistic mishmash of Cambodian and French design. All the automobiles came from the West, as did the latest fashion trends. Suganthini was the most fashionable girl at school, of course. Her long hair and beautiful dresses made her look French, perhaps the highest compliment you could pay someone back then. Each morning she arrived at school from her family's nearby villa in a chauffeured car. Very few people had cars in those days, and no one had a car like the one Suganthini was driven in—an enormous sedan that was bulkier and shinier than any I'd seen before and that barely seemed to fit on the road.

Suganthini's father was the secretary general of Cambodia's Council of Ministers, which made him one of the most powerful people in the country. Her brother-in-law was the commander-in-chief of the armed forces. The family was very rich, with deep connections in the national police and military. It was not a family that a poor Chinese-Cambodian boy held much hope of joining, though that hardly stopped my imagination.

During my first months in Phnom Penh, I admired Suganthini but didn't dare speak to her. The other boys were rich, with powerful families of their own, and the club of privilege seemed closed to me. I occupied myself instead with airy dreams, as well as with school and athletics. I could never stop thinking about Suganthini for long, and I'm certain my grades suffered for it.

Much later, Suganthini told me a story about that time. She was sitting in the courtyard of her family's villa with her mother when the sound of flute notes floated over the wall. "Listen," her mother told her. "Hear that? You can tell whoever is playing is deeply in love." She was a wise woman, though if she knew who the lovebird was she might not have been so enthusiastic. I had learned the flute in middle school, and if I wasn't a virtuoso, I still played with feeling. Not long after the term started, I made the happy discovery that my apartment overlooked the walls of Suganthini's family's house. It seemed like more than a coincidence, like fate had intervened on my behalf, and so each night I sat in the window sending love songs to the girl I was still too scared to speak to and putting my life in fate's hands. Later, gathering my courage, I at last approached her. I had no idea if she knew who I was, but I was sure she had heard my music.

"Have you heard the sound of a flute floating over your walls?" I asked. She was surprised by the question. "I am the flute player," I said simply. She blushed, and I could tell by her reaction she knew how I felt about her.

We began talking, casually at first, in the idle moments between classes, and then as friends, and soon flirtatiously. We began a regular correspondence. Suganthini enlisted one of the maids who looked after her to be our messenger, and we sent notes back and forth. I read each with the eagerness one reads great literature. In one, I lamented that we were never permitted any time to see one another. When we were at school, the teachers enforced a strict code of silence and respect in the class-rooms. Before and after school, she was accompanied by chaperones the family hired to keep an eye on her. At night, she was at home in her villa, which was patrolled by armed guards and where, it was clear, I would not be welcome.

In the note, I asked what would happen if I sneaked into her room at night. She wrote back asking what might happen if, instead of going into her room, I acci-dentally sneaked into her mother's room. She was just joking, aware that no young man in his right mind would try to enter a guarded compound belonging a family of high-ranking officials, the sorts of people who could easily explain away the death of an intruder. What she failed to consider was that I wasn't in my right mind—I was in love.

It rained that night, and I listened to the heavy patter from the window where I normally played the flute. The villa was surrounded by a high wall, and the wall was covered in thick creeping vines. Cambodia's tropical climate and long wet seasons gives rise to thickets of vegetation. During the daytime, I walked around the compound looking for a way in. I sized up a cluster of coconut trees outside the wall. I could see how, after shimmying up the tree, I might swing over to the roof.

From there I could drop down to a veranda and if I was exceedingly lucky, it would be Suganthini's veranda. It was far from a foolproof plan, but I was in no mood to dally. I went back to my room to wait for my opportunity. Late at night, after the rain let up, I set out for the street. Climbing one of the coconut trees, I felt outside of myself. Instinct took over, and before I knew it I was swinging wildly. I landed with barely a sound and stayed where I was for several moments, listening for any sign I had been spotted. The sound I was truly waiting for was the crack of a gun, although it would certainly be the last sound I ever heard. The family owned several dogs, as well, and I was convinced they would give me away. But no sound came.

When I was satisfied no one had noticed, I crept along the veranda. I spotted a nearby window and gave it a pull. To my delight, it opened. Inside, I saw a bathroom. Later, Suganthini would tell me that that bathroom window was ordinarily locked. If it had been locked that evening, I might have been stuck there all night, waiting impatiently for daybreak, when I would meet my end. But fate was still on my side, and I pulled myself through the window into the dark bathroom. The bathroom opened onto a hallway. Here, now, the true folly of my plan came to light. There were ten doors lining the hallway. I had no idea which was Suganthini's and which was her parents'. Entering the wrong room would be suicide.

I prayed for guidance, and I guessed her room was the nearest to the bathroom. I don't know why that room stood out to me—perhaps because it seemed a privileged place, so close to running water, something I had never had, and Suganthini was so deserving of all the luxuries of life. Just as the window to the bathroom was ordinarily closed, the door to this room was usually locked. But on this night, I turned the knob and it yielded. When I opened the door, I slipped inside a dark room. My eyes took a moment to adjust. After they did, I could make out a bed and a figure sleeping. The figure faced away from me, so I couldn't tell who it was. But the hair resting so gently on the pillow was long and black—blacker even than the dark room—and the body seemed to glow with light. I crept inside the room and came around to the side of the bed.

The rain pelted outside the windows, and I kneeled in front of my love. I stayed there for a long time, maybe twenty minutes. It seemed a crime to wake so gentle a creature, and it was a privilege to be there in her presence. Eventually, slowly, I reached out and nudged her shoulder. Her eyes shot open and she seemed ready to scream. Who can blame her? A stranger had sneaked into her room, and for all she knew, I wanted to do her harm.

"It's me," I said urgently. "Please don't scream. If I am caught, your family will kill me."

It took her a moment to figure out who it was she was looking at in the dark room. But she didn't scream, and at last she whispered, "What are you doing here? You must leave. My parents will come, and then the guards will come. You must go."

I told her I wouldn't. "I love you," I said. "If you don't love me, I might as well die. They can kill me right here."

She looked at me for a long time. She was seventeen years old, still a girl, but that beautiful face seemed ageless. At last she nodded. "Very well," she said. "You can stay." Then, nervously, "But what future can we have? What about my father? My mother?" I could not answer such questions, but I had faith things would work out.

Of course, there were logistical problems. Suganthini told me that in the morning a private teacher would come to give her a lesson. We agreed I would hide under the bed while she went downstairs, and I would stay under the bed while the maid cleaned the room. It is preposterous to think of it, but I imagined myself starting a new life in that room. Suganthini would sneak me all the food I needed. What use did I have for fresh air when I could breathe deeply of the love I felt for her? The next day I did hide under the bed, and when the maid girl came, the same one who had helped us pass notes back and forth, I pressed against the ground and barely breathed. She left, and Suganthini and I spent the day together. Fortunately for me, the proximity of the room to the bathroom gave me a chance to relieve myself without being spotted. Day turned into night, and I slept on the floor next to Suganthini's bed. I dared not touch her until I knew her feelings toward me, but to be close to her was exhilarating.

I would stay locked away in Suganthini's room for a month and a half. I paced the room while she was away and I ate sparsely, like a bird, a habit I have maintained and that I believe has kept me healthy to this day. In hindsight, it seems unlikely that I stayed entirely hidden from the house staff. Servants roamed the hallways at all hours, dusting, delivering, and listening. But perhaps out of loyalty to a member of their own class, or out of fear of the consequences of delivering unwelcome news, they kept my secret, and I pleaded my case to Suganthini over days and weeks. She was not convinced of her love for me, though she never asked me to leave. I suspect she was merely waiting the minimum necessary period before revealing her feelings, some gesture of propriety that I, as a poor boy from the country, didn't fully comprehend.

At last, after many days together, she said she did love me, and it was the happiest moment of my life. I had a flair for the dramatic when I was young, and a keen sense for meaningful gestures. In a ceremony, we pricked our fingers and exchanged blood, promising to be faithful to one another for all eternity. Then we made love for the first time, and it felt as if we were joining our souls into one.

•••

We couldn't possibly stay concealed in that bedroom forever, and eventually, we were caught. It was six o'clock in the evening at the end of the firth-fifty day of my seclusion. One of the servants, a girl Suganthini's age, finally confessed to Suganthini's mother that a boy had been hiding in her room. The girl was afraid of being punished if it came to light that she hadn't revealed the truth. The scream downstairs sent shivers up my spine. Her mother called up in a voice meant for the whole house: "Who is in my daughter's room? Who dares sneak into my daughter's room?"

It seemed obvious she wanted me to hear the scream and flee, which would save her an embarrassing confrontation. And flee I did. I threw back Suganthini's window and climbed out onto the roof that had brought me to her weeks earlier. It felt odd to be outside, and I felt exposed so high up in the falling light, as if on display. I leapt for the palm trees and scurried down into the street, and then I ran as fast as I could, certain that the family's private guards were close behind. It wasn't an idle fear. I soon got word that the family was weighing what to do with me. In their eyes, I had violated their daughter, and as an old and respected family they were within their rights to hunt me down and issue a stern punishment. They might even kill me without raising any eyebrows in Phnom Penh. It will seem odd to those reading this in the United States, but that is the order of things in a highly stratified society.

Of course, I felt strongly that Suganthini and I should marry. I was in a tough spot. I couldn't approach her family to explain myself and affirm my love without risking being caught and killed. But I couldn't stay away from my love for long—it would be a fate far worse than whatever punishment her parents might inflict. In hopes of a solution, I called on my mother, who traveled from Sisophon to intercede on my behalf. It was a joy to see her, though I was nervous how everything would play out. When she arrived at the villa, she received a cold welcome from Suganthini's mother. "Please, don't punish my son for being in love," my mother pleaded. But the family was worried about losing face and barely listened to my mother before slamming the door. Fortunately for me, I got my stubbornness from the woman who raised me.

She persisted, going back to the villa each day for two weeks to speak with Suganthini's mother and negotiate on my behalf. After seeing my distress, she begged Suganthini's father to let me see his daughter. They refused many times before at last proposing a solution. I would be allowed one visit with Suganthini. During the visit, I was to renounce my love, tell her I was no good, and explain that she would never see me again. In exchange, the family promised no harm would come to me.

Desperate to see my beloved, no matter the terms, I agreed. An awkward scene ensued, like something out of Shakespeare. We were to meet in a posh room in the home of Suganthini's aunt. To ensure I upheld my end of the bargain, Suganthini's parents would conceal themselves behind a curtain and listen as I ended things with their daughter. A car picked me up. My mother was not permitted to accompany me, so I was all alone and at the mercy of the family. Imagine, then, being a young man in love, being forced to tell the object of your desire that you didn't love her, and knowing full well that the alternative was death. When we got out of the car, my stomach was in knots. It had now been weeks since I'd seen my love, and in her absence, I felt that I was missing some crucial part of myself. Without that organ, I felt I would die. That is how wholly infatuated I was with the beautiful girl with the long black hair.

Suganthini's parents told me where to stand, and then they had servants fetch Suganthini while they hid out of sight. When my love entered, she was even more beautiful than I remembered. She seemed to glow with a special radiance, a combination of her great intelligence, beauty, and miraculous soul. She smiled at me, and I lowered my head in shame. She asked what was wrong. "Suganthini, for a long time I have been hiding from you. I am not a good man. I'm lazy in school, and all my life I have chased girls. For the good of your future, you better listen to your parents and go study in Japan." I repeated the words her parents had told me to say exactly. As they came out of my mouth, they tasted cold and metallic. When I looked up, I saw the pain of what I was saying beginning to break over her eyes. Seeing that pain was too much. I had concealed a dagger in my clothes. The dagger had been a consolation in my time away from Suganthini. I had spent many hours sharpening it, holding it, wondering what the future would hold. Until that moment, I wasn't sure I had the courage to use it.

"It's all a lie. I love you, Suganthini," I proclaimed, in defiance of her parents. I could not bear to lie to her, and if I couldn't be with her, I couldn't bear to live. I withdrew the knife from the folds of my clothes, turned the point toward my stomach, and held my hands out. Then I plunged the blade into my gut. I expected pain, and I was ready for it. If my fate was to die in a demonstration of love, then I could accept that. But there was no pain, only a slowing of time. I could see each curve on Suganthini's face. It was as though she were moving very slowly. I heard her scream out, but the sound was far away. I saw, in the corner of my vision, the curtains draw back, and I watched Suganthini's parents scramble into sight. I found humor in that. I fell to the ground, doubled over now, with blood pooling around me. I watched the scene from above myself, and I felt compassion and an overwhelming sense of love. That is how I know that the final moments of life are not scary. Dying is peaceful, and having come so close that afternoon, I no longer fear it.

I didn't die. Confronted with a young man bleeding to death on their friend's floor, Suganthini's parents summoned an ambulance, which rushed me to the hospital. I was unconscious when admitted, and I stayed in a coma for days. The doctors later told me I was lucky to survive. If I had lost any more blood, I would certainly have died.

In my absence, and not knowing if I would live or not, Suganthini grew despondent. She attempted to kill herself. First she tried to stab herself, but her parents intervened and removed all the scissors and sharp objects from her room. Then she took a handful of pills, but her parents intervened before any damage was done. I had been in the hospital for seven days when I got word that Suganthini was trying to kill herself.

When the doctors let me out, my stomach was full of blood and I was very queasy and weak. But it didn't matter. I went straight to Suganthini's villa and pulled myself up the coconut trees once again. This time, I found that the wall protecting the villa was topped with a double strand of barbed wire. I pulled the strands apart as wide as I could and wormed my way through, but I cut myself very badly, and my clothes became drenched with blood. I had to see Suganthini and to tell her not to kill herself, that we would win in the end. I swung down onto the roof. This time I knew which window was hers. I found her inside, pale as a ghost. But she lit up when she saw me. I told her not to worry, that no force on earth could keep us apart. I told her it was our destiny to be together, and that her parents would see that soon.

Then I reversed my trip, climbing back onto the roof leaping to the fence. This time, I got stuck attempting to pass through the thick barbed wire. Each time I writhed the barbs dug deeper, and I began losing precious blood. Stuck there on the fence like a fish on a hook, I once again believed I would die. I sent up a prayer, and it was answered. Somehow, lunging with the last of my strength, I freed myself. My flesh was torn and the stitches in my stomach had broken. What did it matter? I was in love, and I truly believed we would beat her parents in the end.

I was right. A few days later, after many attempts to convince Suganthini to go to Japan for further studies, her parents finally gave in. The family summoned my mother. She walked in and found Suganthini there, her bags packed. Suganthini's mother told my mother that I had prevailed and that her daughter had made up her mind, despite the family's wishes. We could be together, but she had two conditions. The first was that we not have a wedding ceremony. The shame of having her daughter married off to a poor Chinese-Cambodian was too much for her. The second condition was that we had to promise to go live with my mother in Sisophon, far away from the society gossip and prying eyes of Phnom Penh, where Suganthini was well known.

These were small prices to pay for Suganthini and me to be together, and we readily agreed. We set out for my mother's house the next day, and when we arrived at the humble house in the dusty town of Sisophon, Suganthini only smiled and told me how much she loved me. She didn't need a villa or a chauffeured car. All she needed to be happy was me.

We settled into a quiet life in Sisophon and spent every moment of every day together. Eventually, I'm sure, we would have grown bored, but those months were some of the happiest of my life. Suganthini became pregnant six months after we arrived and sent word back to her mother. The woman's heart had softened with the absence of her daughter, and the thought of missing out on the blessing of a grandchild was too much. After the drama of the previous year, Suganthini's family was ready to mend fences and accept me, a poor young man with few prospects, as their son-in-law. They could see that my love for their daughter was pure, motivated not by a desire for status, but by a bone-deep recognition that I had found my soul mate.

Suganthini and I moved back to Phnom Penh with her family's blessing. We set up a house. Then we prepared to welcome our first child, a boy we called Chet, into the world. That time was so full of love that it would have been impossible for us to predict the horrors that awaited. For a few brief years, we were content.

PART II
OF VI

I HAVE LIVED SO MANY LIVES, BUT PERHAPS NONE SO SWEET as the life Suganthini and I enjoyed in the too-brief years before Cambodia descended into chaos. It amazes me to think how many peaceful years we spent together in Cambodia—they went in a flash—or that I would be thirty-four, long past my impetuous youth, by the time we were forced to flee and start over.

When we moved back to Phnom Penh from our happy temporary exile, Suganthini was six months pregnant with our first son. We rented a small house on the outskirts of the capital. Though Suganthini's family had come to terms with their new son-in-law, they nonetheless wished to keep our love a secret from the gossipy circles of Phnom Penh's elite. We both hurried to finish our degrees at Voltaire School, which we had previously abandoned for love.

After graduating, Suganthini was offered a high-paying job as a schoolteacher. Though she came from great privilege, she never had a complaint about working. I have lived a long time now, and looking back, I can say without reservation that she is the happiest person I have known. Because she was in love, and because she knew how to find the loveliness in all things, she didn't mind a humble life with a poor man like me.

I found work as a tour guide at a travel agency, a job that suited me. Each day I led tours around the capital for foreign visitors. In the 1960s, travelers came from places like the United States, France, and Spain, as well as from nearby countries in Southeast Asia, such as Vietnam and Thailand. Though solitude defined much of my life in school, my old confidence returned now that I had a job and some status. Just as I led bands of children around Sisophon years earlier, I now led troupes of travelers. Many of the visitors were government officials, dignitaries, and wealthy businessmen. We were separated by culture and often by language, but I had a knack for understanding them, for knowing precisely when their attention would waver, when one aspect or another of the city struck them as particularly interesting. It was the emergence of a skill that would serve me well later in life: the ability to read people.

I also had a head for facts and figures, a surprise given my mediocrity in school. I made excellent tip money, and I grew intimately familiar with the changing city. Prince

Sihanouk's grand expansion had made Phnom Penh one of the finest capitals in the region, and I took great pride in showing off the old French architecture alongside the newer buildings, wide boulevards, and proud stone statues.

It was during my first years as a tour guide that I discovered that I also had a talent with languages. My mind absorbed new languages easily, perhaps because I was raised speaking Chinese and had to teach myself Khmer at a young age. I spoke decent French, thanks to my time at Voltaire, and I took every opportunity to practice English and Thai with visitors I led.

One of my great gifts in life, I believe, is that I don't mind looking foolish. I had virtually no fear parading my limited vocabulary in these new languages. I became conversant, and soon quite proficient. It is odd now to see the seeds of my future in that simple job. It also serves as an important lesson: improving yourself is always worthwhile, even if the benefits are not clear to you in the moment. I am alive today because I took the time to learn Thai, and I became rich because I challenged myself to learn English. Education is always worth the investment, and it is a cause that I am committed to promoting now that I am older.

•••

Outside of our happy bubble, Cambodia was entering a troubled period. A 1954 meeting of the world's superpowers in Geneva had delayed the looming conflict between communism and capitalism, but tensions were beginning to boil over, and Southeast Asia had become the flashpoint in an ideological war. The Vietnam War, also known as the second of the Indochina Wars, had been raging since 1955, soon after Vietnam was split into northern and southern zones. The North Vietnamese army was supported by communist allies, including the Soviet Union and China, while the South Vietnamese army was supported by a coalition that included the United States, South Korea, Australia, and Thailand.

Under Prince Sihanouk, Cambodia largely avoided entanglement through the first decade and a half of fighting. The foreign policy at the time could be described as extreme neutrality and noninvolvement. Cambodia had a very small standing army, so diplomacy and wise leadership were essential. Prince Sihanouk did a remarkable job balancing left wing and right wing factions within Cambodia, and in so doing he managed to delay the country's involvement in a brewing regional catastrophe.

But politics inside the country soon began to shift. The North Vietnamese and the communist Viet Cong began taking territory along Cambodia's eastern border. These bases were of enormous strategic importance to them, and the aggressors defended them vigorously. To Cambodia, the presence of Vietnamese soldiers represented an existential threat, an attack on the sovereignty of the nation. Prince Sihanouk was hesitant to attack the

North Vietnamese, because it would upset the balance and thrust Cambodia directly into the escalating war. Tensions within the country grew, and the 1960s saw the rise of right wing hardliners within Cambodia. The 1966 elections swept many of these politicians into office, including a man named Lon Nol, who was elected prime minister under Prince Sihanouk.

Lon Nol had been a loyal advisor to Prince Sihanouk, and he had previously served as defense minister. But views of the two men diverged sharply when it came to the war. While Prince Sihanouk hoped to maintain neutrality, Lon Nol signaled his affinity for the United States and his abhorrence of communism. He was reelected as prime minister in 1968, and his stance against the communists hardened, which he made clear by appointing Prince Sihanouk's cousin, a staunch critic of communists, to serve as his deputy.

In 1970, Prince Sihanouk left the country to tour Europe, the Soviet Union, and China in an effort to reaffirm Cambodia's neutrality and keep the nation out of war. While he was away, massive anti-Vietnam protests erupted in Phnom Penh. The protesters laid siege to the North Vietnamese and Viet Cong embassies. Many now believe the escalation came at the encouragement of Lon Nol. The riots escalated, and with the nation on the brink of turmoil and the president out of the country, Lon Nol and his deputy seized control. Anti-coup demonstrators clashed with anti-Sihanouk demonstrators, and several hundred citizens were killed and thousands more injured.

This was the beginning of the end for Cambodia, which still has not completely recovered from those turbulent years. With Lon Nol in control, the country demanded North Vietnam abandon its bases in Cambodia within seventy-two hours. The bases allowed the North Vietnamese to launch offensive attacks against South Vietnam, and the communists were unwilling to let go of their strategic toeholds along our border.

Meanwhile, the coup had emboldened a communist insurgency within Cambodia, which had been growing slowly over the previous decade. Rather than comply with Lon Nol's demands, the North Vietnamese invaded Cambodia in March of 1970 at the urging of what was then a largely unknown group: the Communist Party of Kampuchea. Soon this group would be known the world over as the Khmer Rouge.

Invasion by the North Vietnamese was a disaster for Cambodia, which had a weak army and was in political disarray following the coup. The North Vietnamese advanced over the eastern border, coming within thirty kilometers of Phnom Penh and quickly capturing more than a third of the country. As North Vietnam took control of large swaths of land, it turned political control over to the Khmer Rouge, which began governing the so-called "liberated" areas while launching attacks against the country's military and political strongholds. Farmers and peasants all around the country joined forces with Khmer Rouge, not because they had any philosophical interest in communism, but because they now associated the government of Lon Nol with the overthrow of Prince Sihanouk, to whom the country's poor were very loyal.

Because of this, the Khmer Rouge soon raised an army of fifty thousand. For those in the Cambodian army, including my brother-in-law, General Sak Sutsakhan, who was overseeing the expansion of the country's national defenses in the early 1970s, peace and neutrality were no longer possible. The government was now fighting a war against North Vietnam while simultaneously fighting a civil war at home.

It was against this chaotic backdrop that I joined the army. I did so at the urging of my brother-in-law. "Ted," he told me, "you speak Thai, Chinese, and French. The nation can use your skills, and you can join as an officer." It was a promising offer. Most citizens joining at that time became infantrymen. After training, they were sent to the front lines to defend the capital. My brother-in-law flattered me by making his appeal seem patriotic. Of course, he likely had other motivations.

By that time, Suganthini and I had a second child, a little girl whom we named Savy. As one of the country's military leaders, a respected soldier, and a politician whom colleagues viewed as incorruptible, my brother-in-law had a clear view of the country's worsening fortunes. As I soon learned, my ability to speak Thai meant I could take my wife and children away from the worst of the fighting. While taking care of the country, my brother-in-law also found time to worry about his loved ones and take care of us as well.

During the long war between communist and anti-communist forces, which gripped Southeast Asia from the 1950s onward, the Thai Royal Government, fearful of communist uprising, became a strong ally of the United States. With Cambodia fighting the communists directly, Thailand began offering support to the Cambodian military. After losing so much land, Cambodia had few facilities left to train recruits, who were volunteering by the thousands. Thailand agreed to offer training to our soldiers and provide military counsel for our leaders.

I was sent to Bangkok to serve as a liaison officer between the Cambodian High Command and the Thai government. My job was to keep the Thai government informed of our activities and to relay messages back to my superiors in Cambodia. I also helped oversee logistics, such as transportation for the trainees. Soldiers came one hundred or 200 at a time to learn to use their weapons and function as a group, and when they were ready to leave, I sent them back to Phnom Penh to protect our homeland. Whenever a high-ranking Cambodian military official came to Bangkok to check on the troops, I picked him up and drove him around, pointing out the sights and showing him the facilities. It was an easy job, and, comically, the skills I used most in the army were those I picked up as a tour guide. The only difference was the hum of war and death, and the threat of an end to Cambodia, which loomed heavily behind everything I did in Thailand.

Often, while interpreting for my brother-in-law, I marveled at the way he made important decisions about troop allocations and strategy. He was decisive, a trait I sometimes saw in myself and that I tried to cultivate after watching him in action. He was also an honest man, and both Cambodia and my growing family were blessed to have him on our side in those gloomy times.

•••

Not long after I arrived in Thailand, and with my brother-in-law's blessing, I sent for Suganthini and the children. We rented a small villa in Bangkok, and though we were right next door to Cambodia, we felt far enough away from the fighting to enjoy a few of the quiet moments of a normal life together. We explored the city, which was more populous and chaotic than Phnom Penh. The noise and the lights made us anxious, though the delicious food was a treat.

Before long I sent for my mother. Incredibly, my father had returned to her after his long absence. He begged her forgiveness and asked that she take him back. My mother was a Buddhist in those days, and well versed in forgiveness after a life in which many wrongs had been done to her. Dreaming of the happy life denied to her by my father's selfishness, she forgave him. But the happy, quiet life she longed for remained elusive now that war had broken out. Eventually she agreed to come live with us in Bangkok. There, at least, I could keep her safe, and together we tried to press on through the drudgery and uncertainty of conflict.

Suganthini and I had another child, a boy we named Chris. He lifted our spirits through the darkest days. Aside from my deep religious faith, no balm in my life can compare to the love of family—a love I would later, to my eternal shame, neglect. In addition to our own growing brood, we took in two older girls and a boy, the children of a friend and a cousin who were struggling in Phnom Penh. In Cambodia, older men are called uncle and older women are called auntie. It is part of our culture that everybody who shows love and demonstrates need becomes a part of your family, and we were happy to be able to provide some safety and stability for the children with so much chaos all around.

I had no grand ambitions at that time, no interest in getting promoted, enriching myself, or pursuing a lofty career. My only thought was of keeping my family safe, and I wanted nothing more than for the war to end so that we could resume our quiet, peaceful life in Phnom Penh, a city that I loved. But that was impossible, and though we didn't realize it at the time, it would not be possible for many years to come. In the capital, the situation had become grave. Each month, I traveled back on a military airplane to collect payroll for the officers stationed in Thailand and check in with my superiors. Each month, I saw conditions deteriorate.

By 1974, the sound of gunfire was audible on the outskirts of the capital, which was encircled by fighting. The Khmer Rouge continued to recruit from the country-side and with support from the North Vietnamese, the enemy outnumbered and outgunned our national army. Rockets and bombs lit up the sky, and citizens lived in fear that Phnom Penh would be overrun any day. It was jarring to go from that hellish scene to Bangkok, where my family and I lived peacefully, and I gave thanks for the foresight General Sak Sutsakhan had to get us out of the country when he did. His gift to us was the gift of safety and security, and it is one I have never forgotten.

In April 1975, just before the Cambodian New Year, life as we knew it ended. My mother missed Sisophon terribly. Aside from my prodigal father, she missed my sisters and wanted to visit them. The Cambodian New Year is normally a time of celebration; it is especially a time to be with loved ones, and my mother insisted on returning to Cambodia for a few days. She promised she would come back to Bangkok soon and eventually, in the face of her insistence, I consented.

Meanwhile, I had to travel to Phnom Penh to update my superiors. I loved my home very much, but the visits to Cambodia were becoming dangerous. Just before I left,

I received word that the US embassy had withdrawn its staff from Phnom Penh—an ominous sign. The country's acting head of state had also left, citing health reasons. On April 12, my brother-in-law, who had been working tirelessly to stave off the advancing communist troops, was appointed the new acting head of state in his place. There was no man on earth better suited for the job, and though his tenure would be short, Cambodia can be proud that it had such a competent, capable man leading the country in its time of need.

On April 15, I flew on a military transport from Bangkok to Phnom Penh. When I arrived, I reported to the officers and quickly dispatched my duties. Then I went to call on my in-laws, taking a car to the part of the city where Suganthini grew up. It was hard to believe that the villa where the chauffeur dropped me was the same one I had sneaked into years earlier. I had changed. I was no longer a child, but a respectable young man with a wife and three children. I walked into the main house with my head held high. The house had changed, too. The palatial home that had so impressed me as a youth now seemed heavy with anxiety. It was clear that my in-laws were nervous. The rooms were in disarray, as if someone had been packing in a hurry, and most of the servants had gone.

My visit was quick and cordial, and after exchanging some warm words with Suganthini's parents I went back to the airfield to catch a plane to Bangkok. I was in for a bad surprise. A young airman told me there was no plane to take me back to Thailand. At the height of the war, planes left every hour, so it seemed strange that there was no transport scheduled for takeoff. I returned to my in-laws' house to wait, but the day passed, and still there were no planes scheduled. I began to grow nervous. Finally, on the afternoon of April 16, one day after the New Year, I got a phone call from one of my contacts in the air force. As a liaison officer, I had many friends, and I have always found that a good friend is far more valuable than money in times of need. My contact told me that there was a plane leaving in just a few minutes. And he told me something else, which still chills me to remember. He said it would likely be the last transport out of Cambodia. The capital would soon fall. If I wasn't on that plane, I would be left behind. We both had a good idea what that meant. To be a military officer in enemy-occupied territory is often a death sentence, and even though we didn't know the true nature of the Khmer Rouge at that point, we suspected that this enemy was worse than most.

My father-in-law drove me to the airport in a rush. I had earned his respect, in large part because he saw how happy I made his daughter and how willing I was to work to give her a comfortable life. The war likely helped our relationship. Desperate times have a way of tearing down artificial divisions between people. A rich man caught in war sees that he can lose everything very quickly, and that changes his perspective. Now he was flying down the wide boulevards of central Phnom Penh's empty roads to try to help me escape. Rockets were falling intermittently on the city, and very few people were outside.

The airport was under bombardment when we arrived. The Khmer Rouge and the North Vietnamese still hadn't entered Phnom Penh, but they were just outside the city and targeting valuable military assets. When we arrived, I leapt from the car, turning to wave to my father-in-law. We exchanged a look, and though I had no way of knowing what was to come, I knew what his expression meant: *Protect my daughter, take care of her, take care of my grandchildren.* I nodded. And then we parted.

An American cargo plane was idling on the runway. It had just dropped off the last American provisions in support of the failing defense effort. The plane's propellers were spinning and it was ready to take off. My friend in the air force had delayed it for me. With my small bag in hand, I darted across the runway. The long strip of concrete was chewed up in places where rockets had hit, and as I ran, I felt the percussion of an explosion some-where off to my right. The Khmer Rouge was supplied by the North Vietnamese, and their weapons were first rate. When I neared the plane, I saw the pilot waving me on frantically from the cockpit. I bounded up the stairs, which closed behind me. The pilot wasted no time. The plane began rolling down the runway, slowly at first, and then with great speed. A rocket struck near our section of runway, and we all held our breath. A direct hit would mean a fiery death.

The plane lurched for what seemed like an eternity. Time moves slowly when your life is under threat. I had time to think of my children and my wife. I wasn't scared for myself, but the thought of leaving them alone with no country and no husband terrified me. At last I felt the weight against my chest: liftoff. I closed my eyes and we ascended into the warm April air.

There were no windows near me in the cargo plane, but if there had been I would have looked down at the city I loved and the country I would not see again for many years. I would have said goodbye. From the air, I might have seen the circle of communist troops tightening like a noose around one of the finest capital cities in Southeast Asia. It was the closest I would come to the Khmer Rouge. My friends, my family, and, I now believe, God himself all worked together to save me.

•••

We landed in Bangkok and I went to find Suganthini and tell her I was okay, that the capital would soon fall. Word had already spread on the radio that defeat was imminent. Now that I was back safely, our thoughts turned to Suganthini's brother and parents, and to my mother, who had returned to Cambodia for the New Year celebration. General Sak Sutsakhan, as acting head of state, spent the last day of the Republic doing what he could to secure a conditional ceasefire.

But reason held no sway for the Khmer Rouge. The group's ruthless leader, Saloth Sar, wanted absolute victory. On the morning of April 17, 1975, communist troops entered the capital. Saloth Sar, a longtime member of the Khmer communist movement and a man largely unknown internationally, assumed control. In the years to follow his infamy would spread, though he would be better known by his adopted *nom de guerre*: Pol Pot.

As the capital fell, my brother-in-law rushed his family to Phnom Penh's National Stadium, which had become a staging ground for the Cambodian armed forces. Accompanying him was the Cambodian prime minister, Long Boret. The two had spent the last weeks in intense negotiations with leaders around the world and with the Khmer Rouge, and both were weary. The acting head of state, along with his wife and four children, climbed aboard the last Khmer Air Force helicopter, but Long Boret's family had not arrived yet, and he demanded that the helicopters wait. Khmer Rouge soldiers had already entered the stadium and were shooting at the helicopters. My brother-in-law told him they could not wait.

Just as the helicopter was taking off, Long Boret spotted his family driving into the stadium in a truck. He leapt off the helicopter and ran to them. The group ran to another waiting chopper, but when the pilot tried to start it, it would not work. The helicopter was old and broken, a tragic metaphor for the state of the Cambodian army. Long Boret was apprehended and executed later that day.

It was less than a day after my flight out of Phnom Penh, but it seemed to all of us to be a year. With no other helicopters or planes taking off, my mother-in-law and father-in-law stayed behind. Though we didn't learn their fate for many years, we later discovered that Suganthini's parents were executed immediately by the invading troops, part of the first round of executions of members of the ruling class. It was prelude to the senseless atrocity ahead, which so many of my countrymen would endure for years. Their swift deaths were, in a strange way, a mercy. To be rich, educated, and part of the old power structure in Pol Pot's Cambodia meant torture and a painful execution, and it is some comfort all these years later to know that they escaped the depths of that brutality, which would see three million slaughtered, with the quick death of a few bullets.

With Cambodia in the hands of the communists, I, along with the thousands of others who escaped, were now officially refugees. It is a frightening thing to realize that there is no home to return to. We had been in Bangkok for four years already, and though we never felt entirely comfortable there, it had become our home. But with the Cambodian military defeated and dissolved, there was no reason to stay. As a military liaison, I had many contacts at the Cambodian embassy and within the

Thai government. I spent the first harried weeks after the fall of the Republic helping Cambodians in Thailand find settlement around the world. The Cambodian embassy coordinated with countries like the United States, France, and Canada. When we found settlement for someone, I helped arrange transportation. We sent them to U-Tapao Air Base in the southern portion of Bangkok. U-Tapao had been a sleepy airport in the 1960s, but when America entered the Vietnam War, it helped build massive runways to support the B-52s that supplied its troops. Now the airport was an international hub, with several flights each day to the West and a large contingent of American troops permanently stationed there.

After a stay in U-Tapao, the Cambodian nationals boarded transports and flew halfway around the world to their new homes. Many of the refugees were wealthy, which allowed them to escape the country in the first place. But in their haste to flee, most left behind all but their most prized possessions. Now many of them would have to start new lives in new countries. Cambodians are resourceful and enduring, and we have always prided ourselves on being hardworking. The first wave of refugees following the Cambodian civil war would have to call on those skills and carry the flag of our fallen country as they stepped into an uncertain future.

After weeks of long days helping resettle others, a friend in the embassy at last told me there was nothing more I could do. Without a task to occupy my every waking minute, our new reality began to dawn on me. I worried for my mother, whom I had no way to contact, and for my in-laws, whom we hoped, naively, were still alive. Mostly I worried for my children, for the uncertainty of the world they lived in. We were still looking after my adopted nephew and two nieces, so we were a large clan. I resolved to support my family through these dark times, no matter what.

Suganthini, the children, and I went to U-Tapao. The base was comfortable, with new amenities built to house the American soldiers. We were treated kindly by the people there, given wholesome meals, and made to feel welcome. Because of our uncertain status, we were confined to an area set aside for refugees, and it was a strange feeling not to have the freedom to come and go as we pleased. The country had fallen so quickly, and relatively few people had escaped. In total there were between ten thousand and twenty thousand refugees in need of host countries.

We spent a month at the base. At first, our emotions expressed themselves in primary colors: fear, relief, anxiety, sadness. But over the course of that idle month, we felt the subtler shades of grief and gratitude. Suganthini, my beautiful wife, was a source of comfort to the children and me. She had lost more than anyone—her status, her wealth, and perhaps many members of her family. She suffered and felt great sadness, but she did so with heavenly grace and dignity.

In the air base, the children made up games and spent hours running around the refugee area. There were many families, all of them afraid, but we made the best of the situation. The men talked about politics and war, which is what men talk about to come to terms with complex realities they can't fully grasp. The women looked after the children and comforted each other. A sort of community developed, one born of shared hardship.

The refugees in the camp were assigned to various host countries with help from the Cambodian embassy. Because of my work as a liaison officer, I was appointed president of the camp and so could help assign people to their new homes. Aside from the country where they would land, however, none of us knew anything specific about what the future held. When refugees landed on military bases in their host countries, they would be processed and given further instructions. Suganthini's brother-in-law had arrived in the air base before us, and he and his family were sent to Pennsylvania.

After a month sleeping on cots, we received word that a transport plane bound for Camp Pendleton in Southern California had room for our large group. Those words—Southern California—meant little to me. We knew next to nothing about the United States, although we knew it to be a place of freedom and prosperity. At that time, the differences between the states were abstract. Later, I felt it was a great stroke of fortune that we were brought to so beautiful a place as California.

•••

The plane ride was long and uncomfortable, but we felt happy to be flying away from the chaos and heartbreak of Southeast Asia. When we touched down at Camp Pendleton, we were taken to the barracks that would be our new temporary home. Then we were given food, my first American meal. I don't recall what it was, but I do vividly remember eating on American soil with my family while the California sun warmed the earth outside. The quality of light seemed different than in Cambodia, a honey-color I had never seen before. It was a beautiful sun, and it gave me hope.

To stay in the country as refugees, we needed sponsors. Aside from those travelers I had encountered as a tour guide years earlier, we didn't know any citizens. We were told not to worry—charitable groups had been following the atrocities in Cambodia and were signing up to sponsor refugees. In the meantime, we were free to leave the base during the day. We visited the city of Oceanside a few times. The city sits directly south of Camp Pendleton and, as the name implies, is situated along a pristine stretch of the Pacific Ocean. Looking west, the water looked very different to us. Cambodia is situated on the Gulf of Thailand, and the open Pacific seemed much grander and more vast than any water I had ever seen. It made us feel very small. Across that immense ocean was our home, our friends, and our relatives.

We had no money, so we didn't take more than a couple trips off base. There were other Cambodian refugees waiting for sponsorship and processing, and the same sense of community that had helped us through U-Tapao took hold at Camp Pendleton. The base permitted visitors, and some of the other refugees had family members who had already been placed in Southern California or emigrated years earlier as students or businessmen.

When these visitors came, they brought money, delicious food, and good cheer. In fact, it seemed to me that most of the other refugees received visitors, which made my wife and children feel even more alone in this new place. We knew no one in California, and we had no way of contacting Suganthini's brother-in-law in Pennsylvania. We didn't even have enough money for a phone call. Once more we felt an odd mix of emotions. We were so happy to be in California, but we were uncertain about the future. It was a heart-wrenching month, and as I did many times in those days, I resolved to build my family a life of comfort and peace, no matter what.

At last we received word: someone had volunteered to sponsor us. Our saviors belonged to a church in the city of Tustin in Orange County. We were Buddhists at the time, but it hardly mattered to the good people at Peace Lutheran. We were souls in need, and they went far out of their way to provide for us. After seeing so many other refugees receive visitors throughout our stay, our metaphorical adoption by Peace Lutheran was thrilling. Finally, somebody wanted us.

I remember that day so clearly. Three large American cars came to pick us up. The cars in the United States were much larger than those in Asia, and it felt like we were participating in a very important procession. We met the pastor of the church and some members who had volunteered to pick us up. My English was passable, but very rough, and at the time no one else in my family spoke the language. But the warmth of the people in the car transcended language, and we were comforted by that.

The church rented us a home in Tustin. It was a beautiful little house, with three bedrooms and modern amenities. The differences between the standard of living in the United States and Cambodia became apparent when Suganthini attempted to make a meal. A church aid had stocked the refrigerator with food, but as Suganthini went to prepare dinner, she realized she had no idea how the American stove and oven worked. It was a comical scene watching her twisting knobs and pushing and pulling on what might have been buttons. At last we scrounged together some ingredients from the fridge that the children could eat cold, and we had our first meal in our new home. The next day, when representatives from the church came back, we asked for help and got a primer on using an American stove.

The church generously paid our rent with no discussion of us paying the money back. Additionally, they gave me a job tending the grounds and cleaning the facilities at Peace Lutheran. With limited English, there wasn't much else I was qualified to do. Each day I rode a bicycle to the church. The streets of Tustin were so quiet compared to the streets we were used to in Thailand and Cambodia. We had lived in congested cities, but Tustin was a spacious suburban community with many affluent residents. The houses were nicely spaced and at times the roads seemed to have no cars on them at all. The biggest difference was that there were hardly any people on the streets. Americans, we quickly found out, preferred to drive than walk or ride bikes.

At the church, I mowed the grass with a riding mower and cleaned up the yard. When the parishioners left, I swept and emptied the trashcans. Though they were already paying our rent, the church gave me another $500 per month for my labor. It seemed like a lot of money, but we soon discovered that everything in California was more expensive than we were used to. With eight mouths to feed, it was imperative I find additional work.

One of the church officials was named Dean Beaumon. He was a kind, gentle man who went out of his way to help my family and me. "Dean," I said one day, "I don't think $500 is enough to feed my family. I'd like to find another job." My nieces and nephew were older than my children. Along with my wife, I knew they could handle the work at the church. "I have the manpower," I explained. "If they take care of the church, I can spare myself to work on something else part time to bring in extra money."

Dean thought about it and said he agreed. He put some calls out, and soon I had a second job working evenings as an attendant at a Mobil station on Tustin Avenue. My hours were 10:00 p.m. to 6:00 a.m., and when I got home I went to the church to help with the grounds work. It was exhausting, but I soon learned I could train myself to work long hours and not grow overly tired, a skill that would help me down the road. The Mobil station was some distance from our house, so Dean taught me to drive, helped me get my license, and gave me an old car. Driving to work, I felt like a proper American.

The gas station was very busy on Friday and Saturday nights as people went out to eat and socialize, but during the week it was quiet. Though I didn't realize it at the time, watching traffic patterns from my perch at the gas station would soon become a very useful skill. The station always kept two night attendants on duty. I worked with a very nice man named Andy. By speaking with him during slow weeknights, my English soon improved. One evening, after we'd gone more than an hour without seeing a single customer, he said, "Ted, have you ever had a donut?" Anybody who's has ever learned another language knows that the words for foods are tricky. I had never heard of a donut. "Tell you what," he said, seeing the quizzical look on my face. "Watch the station for a minute. I'm going to go grab some for us."

He ran across the street to a small shop with an illuminated sign out front. A few minutes later he came back with a pink box, which he opened toward me. I took out a puffy, glazed ring of airy dough and took a small bite. "Wow," I exclaimed. A feeling of nostalgia passed over me. In Cambodia, we have a rice flour pastry called *nom kong*. Chewing the donut, I was transported back to childhood celebrations and sweet moments with my mother, who occasionally brought sweet treats home for me. When my shift ended at 6:00 a.m. the next morning, I went to the twenty-four-hour shop and bought a dozen more donuts. Then I drove home and shared them with my family. I was a hero to my young kids.

Back at the gas station, I began watching the donut shop and noticing how busy it got at certain hours. Though the donuts themselves were inexpensive, I watched customer after customer march in and come back out with full bags and cups of coffee. When the shop was slow, people lingered inside reading the newspaper or chatting. I began to form an idea. One evening, during a slow stretch, I walked over to the shop. It was run by two women. One woman made the donuts and the other tended to customers. The woman at the serving window was handing coffee to a police officer. I waited until she finished, and then stood in front of her. In my best English, I said, "Listen, I want to know what you think. If I can raise $3000, would it be enough to open a little shop like this?"

The woman had a big personality and spoke very loudly. "No way! Are you crazy? You'll throw your money away. You don't know how to pick a location. You don't know the business. You'll lose all your savings!"

I must have looked a bit dejected.

"But hon, why don't you try Winchell's?" she offered. "They hire people all the time, and they have a training program. They'll even give you your own store."

I didn't know what Winchell's was, but the name sounded impressive, almost regal. I thanked the woman, bought some day-old donuts, and went back to work. When I got home that morning, I gave the donuts to my family, our new weekly tradition. When I told Suganthini about the interaction, she said, "I've seen one of those Winchell's. It's not far from the house."

I visited the shop, which was clean, well lit, and very well organized. I asked the man behind the counter for an application and information about the training program. He looked me up and down before informing me that I needed to go to the regional headquarters in La Mirada. The next day, when Dean Beaumont came to check up on us, and I asked if he would come with me to the La Mirada headquarters.

"Ted," he said, "I wouldn't get your hopes up. That's a management position, and they're not likely to hire someone who doesn't have a US education."

"Dean," I said, "please, let's try."

"You think you can convince them?" he asked.

"I do," I said, with unearned confidence.

Dean agreed, and when we arrived, we found the regional manager. I introduced myself, and then Dean began to say a lot of nice things about me. He told the man that I was an officer in the army in Cambodia, that I spoke Thai, French, and English, in addition to Khmer, and that I was a hard worker and very responsible. The manager thought for a moment. Then he looked at Dean and said, "Do you guarantee this man is responsible and that he will be a good employee for Winchell's?"

Dean didn't hesitate. "I guarantee it," he said.

"All right, that's good enough for me. Ted, when can you start?"

"I can start right now," I said. "I'm ready."

The man chuckled, and then invited me to the back to begin filling out paperwork.

That is how I entered the donut business. There wasn't a person alive, myself included, who could have predicted where it would take me.

MY ROAD TO BECOMING A MILLIONAIRE STARTED WITH A TRAINEE badge. Winchell's was an excellent company to work for. The training curriculum was rigorous, requiring potential managers to perform every job in the factory-like, high-volume donut operation. Each night, I returned home to Suganthini and my family hungry and exhausted. For $500 a month, I cleaned every inch of the store, handled money, and baked each donut on the menu. I opened and closed, and I did the thousand little things that must be done to keep a store running and customers happy.

My English improved rapidly, and with my experience as a tour guide, I was a quick study learning to deal with customers. I remember the puzzled expressions on the faces of early customers as they strained to understand what I was saying. Like many second-language learners, I could always understand others better than I could express myself, so those early interactions were amusing for both sides. I would say something in my heavy Cambodian accent, and they would take a few moments to parse what I meant. Then they would respond in a slow approximation of English, the kind a good-natured adult might use with a child. Eventually our interactions began to pick up, both because my skills improved and because my regular customers began to understand my accent. I took great joy in discovering new depths and levels of sophistication in my customers.

Baking was another question. If I didn't know a word while in conversation, I could easily skip over it or guess my partner's meaning. But each word in a recipe is crucial, and the timing and measurements must be precise. Donuts are not particularly difficult to make—you mix dry ingredients in the bucket of a stand mixer, add wet ingredients, and follow the steps. A third grader with knack for staying on task could handle most of the job, provided someone was willing to help with the backbreaking job of lifting sacks of donut mix and hefting the finished dough onto the cutting table. But the instructions seemed inscrutable to me at first. Though I excelled at most of the work right away, it took me longer to master baking, and more than a few trays of my early donuts had to be discarded before they reached the shelves, having missed some crucial step in the proofing or baking stages.

The woman who told me about the Winchell's training program had done me a tremendous favor—despite calling me crazy. It was clear after a few weeks of training that without specialized knowledge of the business, there is no way I would be able to set up my own location. At best, I would make several costly mistakes, and at worst I would squander what little money my family and I had managed to save in an endeavor doomed to end in failure. Luck favors the bold, but only if they're adequately prepared. Aside from the specifics of making and selling donuts, there were all manner of small business techniques I had never had to learn in Cambodia, such as balancing books and tallying receipts, handling payroll, managing employee schedules, and paying bills. Thanks to the training program, I learned the business, had a chance to make all the mistakes, and got to take home a salary at the same time.

And there was another benefit to receiving training from Winchell's. Most donut stores at that time were mom-and-pop shops, and the quality of the donuts between one shop and the next varied tremendously. Most shop owners opted to save money by buying inferior ingredients. With few employees—some shops had just two—they chose to bake donuts once in the morning and serve the same batch all day, which resulted in a stale product by the afternoon. Winchell's was different. The company brought the same efficiency and dedication to making quality donuts that the McDonald's brothers and Ray Kroc originally brought to cooking burgers and fries. The donuts were consistently fresh, which is why customers loved them, and the chain used the highest quality ingredients, keeping prices low by buying in bulk for dozens of stores at a time. For me, it was an education not only in donut making but also in the art of appealing to customers. I experienced first hand the pride that came with knowing you were offering your customers superior service, and it was always delightful when people took the time to tell me how much they enjoyed a donut I had ushered into existence.

When I graduated from the program, Winchell's gave me a store to manage on Balboa Pier in the Newport Peninsula. It was a small shop serving a mix of tourists and regulars, and the volumes were low. Still, I took tremendous pride in being a manager, and I ran a tight ship. Donuts are simple, sweet treats, but running a donut shop is a lot of hard work. Once more, I stayed up each night baking. Often I would carry Chris, my youngest son, from our home to the shop. While it was still very dark, I would lay Chris beside the big cutting table where I worked the dough into donut-sized portions. He slept soundly, gathering a light coating of flour as I labored through the night. I had learned to do with very little sleep working at back at the gas station, and that skill served me well in my new career, as it would for years to come.

We decided to move out of the house that Peace Lutheran had generously rented us and relocated to an apartment near the pier, which became the center of our universe. As any small-business owner knows, days are consumed by small worries and you end up spending most of your time at work. Ingredients had to be ordered, contracts fulfilled or negotiated, and maintenance issues dealt with before the first customers walked through the door.

•••

Suganthini helped me run the Balboa Pier shop. She arrived early in the morning to make the coffee and take care of the customers. She seemed to glow when she interacted with people, and her warmth was infectious. I remember distinctly the face of a customer that many patrons found unpleasant. He would come into the shop in a foul mood, which radiated off him like electricity. After several interactions with him, I began to sigh whenever he came in. My duty was to serve my customers, but the man always left me feeling sour. But I noticed that whenever Suganthini greeted him, he melted into a chatty, humble person. The transformation was incredible, and I witnessed it many times in those early years in America.

There is a tendency in any culture to be wary of people who look different than you do, and in the 1970s, not many people in Newport Beach had met a single person from Cambodia. But everybody who came near Suganthini loved her immediately, and because of her magnetism and kindness, we felt like part of the community.

During those early days in the shop, my wife once again demonstrated her resiliency. The work was difficult, the pay quite low, but she did it with a smile. I realized early on that it would be important to develop excellent relationships with my customers, and in that way I got my first real taste of what it meant to be an American. I would chat with men about sports and with women about the gossip around town. I learned a great deal about life in my new homeland. I also made several friends. As a young man, I never had strong friendships. In part this is because I moved so often throughout school and had to fend for myself, but in part I think it is because I am better suited to managing, which stands in the way of close friendship. But I have always valued the bonds I form with people, and my customers gave me a great gift by allowing me to engage with them socially and enjoy the easy closeness of daily interaction.

One day, one of my regular customers came in with a copy of the *Orange County Register*. He was a policeman, and he and I chatted most mornings before he returned to his beat. I had mentioned to him that my dream was to open a shop of my own one day, and he encouraged me to act as soon as possible. On this morning, he gave me an unexpected push.

"Hey Ted," he said, a wide smile on his face. "Look at this." He slid the newspaper over to me. He had circled a classified ad in pen: Donut shop for sale. "You ought to go down there and see what they want for it."

It was a bold idea. I hadn't thought of looking for a shop of my own so soon. With my family working at the church, and with Suganthini helping at the Winchell's, we had saved some money. But I didn't have nearly enough to buy the shop without taking out a loan, which would be risky. Still, we were in the land of opportunity, and there is no reward without risk. I called the owners and arranged a meeting. Suganthini covered the store while I drove out to the city of La Habra. The shop was small and located on a quiet street. It was a pleasant, clean store, though compared to the high standards of Winchell's everything inside seemed a bit old and rundown. Like many small restaurants and shops in Southern California, the front was a tall steeple of glass held up on one central stilt. A few customers were enjoying donuts and coffee at tables inside when I went in and introduced myself.

The owner was an old man named Mr. Christensen. He had owned the location for many years, and he and his wife were ready to retire. They hoped to pass the store off to someone they could trust and who would continue to serve the customers with whom they had become friendly over the years. We spoke for a long time. I told him about my family and myself, and I related the story of our arrival in America. He was a good man, and he considered himself a good judge of character. When he saw I was a serious person, he told me it would make him very happy to sell me the shop. We spoke about price. He wanted $40,000, which included all equipment. The new owner would take over the shop's lease, which was locked in at a set rate for several years. I reviewed his books and saw that the shop was sleepy, earning between $30,000 and $40,000 in profit every year, which was just enough for a husband and wife team. We negotiated a little, settled on a price, and came up with terms for a loan. I would give him a down payment, and Mr. Christensen offered to give me a note.

After we agreed in principle on the main aspects of the deal, I rushed back to my Winchell's to tell Suganthini the news. She was ecstatic. I have never met a person who exudes so much emotion, and it was always a joy for me to bring her good news. We had suffered much in the last few years, so every smile from her was a mercy.

"What's the name of the shop?" she asked.

"They call it Christy's," I told her.

That name would play a large role in our lives going forward. Suganthini, tired of correcting customers who couldn't pronounce her name, would soon adopt it as her own, the last symbolic step in her transformation into a proper American. I had fallen in love with a girl who smelled like flowers. My love kept growing, and I was so thankful for the woman who came home smelling of sweet donuts.

Christy's was the first thing that was ours in America. Owning something in this country was especially significant to us because of all we had lost when we were forced out of Cambodia. At last, after a long delay, we felt like we were building a life instead of just surviving. Anybody who has crossed that threshold one or more times knows the pride and satisfaction the journey from desperation to self-sufficiency holds.

To ensure a smooth transition, Mr. Christensen and I came up with a plan. I would work with the Christensens for one month, and they would tell customers they hired me to give them a hand. In that way, I could learn the ropes of the location and get to know the patrons without startling anyone. Ownership changes can be shocking for customers, and if Suganthini and I were going to be successful with the new location, we needed to keep the loyal business the Christensens had built up over the years.

Both Suganthini and I felt a sense of loyalty to Winchell's. Cambodians are loyal people—it is a trait that means a lot to us culturally. In our country, to betray someone is considered about the worst thing you can do. Winchell's had given me a tremendous gift, paying for my training before giving me one of its shops to run. It felt wrong to walk away from that gift in my first year. Leaving the guaranteed paycheck also felt like a big gamble—too big, in fact, considering I had a large family to support.

So Suganthini and I decided to keep the Winchell's store and run Christy's simultaneously. It was the smart decision, though it entailed making some big sacrifices. If we thought we were working hard before, our lives would soon become a lesson in the limits of human endurance.

•••

When my month of training with the Christensens began, I worked hard to master all the recipes. That was important, because customers had grown used to the donuts at Christy's. Even if most donut recipes are very similar, small tweaks here and there, like how often the oil in the fryer is changed or how long the dough is left to proof, can account for big changes in flavor. The donut is a simple food made from just a few ingredients. But go to any three donut shops and order the same kind of donut and you'll begin to understand that they hide a surprising amount of complexity and nuance. While I worked with the Christensens learning the ropes, Suganthini ran the shop in Newport. After my training, I would return to Newport to bake and clean.

There was an odd advantage to working so hard. Living in sunny California with eighteen hours of work each day, we had very little time to think about what was happening back in Cambodia. The Vietnam War ended in 1975 when US troops pulled out. After that long, bloody period, the West had little appetite for ongoing troubles in Southeast Asia. There were few news reports about the situation in Cambodia, and with our friends and surviving family members either spread out all over the world or trapped inside a brutal dictator's borders, we had little sense what was happening. With so much work, we could forget, even if just for a few hours at a time, the devastating shock that had befallen our nation.

When the month was over, the Christensens announced to their customers that I would be taking over. By that time, I had built up a lot of goodwill, and the customers knew my face. The Christensens handed over the keys, gave their shop one last look, and then wished me good luck. They were happy to be leaving, and looking forward to their retirement, but I also saw a note of sadness as they left the business they had built.

I understood. They had toiled over the fryer and cash register for years, and now they were saying goodbye to a thing they had created. No matter how ready they were, there was sadness in their eyes as they walked out into the parking lot and ducked into their old car. Later, they would stop by to visit occasionally. I was always happy that they seemed satisfied with the way things were going.

I kept most things exactly as they were while implementing a few key changes I learned from Winchell's. I began baking the donuts in small batches throughout the day. Aside from ensuring they were always fresh, which encouraged customer loyalty, the smell of donuts baking became its own form of advertising. It was far more effective than a huge sign or a sandwich board.

There are few things that smell better than a tray of hot donuts cooling in the rack, and a good portion of our foot traffic came from people passing by who suddenly caught a whiff of our delicious confections.

In addition to baking more frequently, I swapped out the ingredients the Christensens were using with higher quality ingredients, the kind I used at Winchell's. They cost a little more, but the price was easy to justify. Customers began to comment on how good the donuts had become, and the solid business the Christensens had built began to pick up even more.

With the income from Winchell's and the income from Christy's, Suganthini and I made about $40,000 our first year as donut shop owners. I trained my nephew to bake, and he helped at the La Habra store. One of our advantages as immigrants was that we had a household of people willing to work hard to make a living. Because of the language barrier, and lacking Western degrees, there weren't many opportunities for my nephew or nieces, so they were glad for the work.

We earned enough money to provide for our family and put a little in savings, and we were happy to have the stability. But we also saw that we had quickly maxed out our earning potential at the two shops. At best, we could hope to add a few thousand per year by growing our customer base. We were working long days with no breaks and no possibility of vacations, so the stability came at quite a cost.

In the great American tradition, I decided the only way we would improve our quality of life was to expand. Now that I had a grasp on the donut business, I thought it would theoretically be possible to acquire more shops and train employees to do the hard work. In truth, I had no idea if it would be a profitable model. But I kept my eyes open and early in 1977, I saw another ad in the *Register*. This one was in the city of Fullerton. I decided to do a little investigating before approaching the owners, so I drove out and sat in my car opposite the shop. It was like a stakeout in the movies. I could immediately see the location was far superior to both the Christy's and the Newport Peninsula Winchell's. The shop was situated on a busy street near a freeway off-ramp, which was a good sign. The busiest time in the donut business is during the morning rush, when commuters on their way to work stop by to grab a coffee and some quick breakfast. The old real estate maxim is very true when it comes to selling donuts: the name of the game is *location, location, location.*

Because the Fullerton shop was high-volume, the price was much higher than the La Habra location: $100,000. But it came with a good long-term lease, which meant the largest cost—the rent—was predictable for several years to come. This was crucial. If I knew how much rent was, and if I could estimate the volume, I could come up with an accurate model for how much money

I stood to make. I met with the owner and we negotiated a down payment.

It's often easier to get a note from a mom-and-pop owner, which may seem counterintuitive. Usually they are getting out of the business to enjoy their retirement, and they often prefer a steady monthly sum paid over a long period, which replaces their income. If I were to default, they could simply take the store back and sell it to someone else. The risk to them is very low.

With the deal in place, I scrambled to execute my big plan. So often in business of any kind, the best way to make money is to help other people make money. That was my philosophy when I approached a Cambodian family we knew and offered to lease them Christy's. With a few grown children, the husband and wife had a ready labor force, but little opportunity to make money. Most immigrants at the time ended up working at places like McDonald's for three dollars an hour. Christy's was bringing in between $20,000 and $30,000 in profit per year. The family was ecstatic at the opportunity, and we came to terms on a deal. They would pay me a down payment from their savings, and I would lease them the turnkey shop for a fixed price every month. I decided that a fair lease price would be roughly one-third the profit. I would train the family myself, and if they worked hard, they stood to make a reliable income of $20,000 or more per year, which was far more than they were making as fast food employees.

As an added benefit, they would be their own bosses and wouldn't have to answer to a manager.

There is no better gift you can offer refugees who have had their lives ripped away and their circumstances dictated to them by outside forces. Americans are used to having opportunities, so it may not be entirely clear to them how rare and special those opportunities are. But the American dream is more than a publicity slogan. It is a beacon of hope for people around the world who are desperate and suffering under unjust conditions. The Cambodian family's success depended entirely on the work ethic of its members. In addition to being loyal, Cambodians are very hard workers, so I was confident they would prosper.

When I took over the Fullerton shop, I also spent part of my time training the husband and wife back at Christy's, eventually handing over the keys to the new managers. I remembered the day Winchell's gave me the keys to the Balboa Pier shop. More than a mere job, it felt like I was once again a man who could provide for his loved ones. My attachment to that small shop may be another reason I held on to it long after I had enough money to hand back the keys.

With Christy's leased out, I now had about $1,000 per month in recurring income, and after we finished training, I didn't have to do any additional work aside from making myself available for advice. It was guaranteed cash every month, and it validated the model I had dreamed up. I saw clearly that there was a path to expand in the same way, perhaps adding as many as a dozen shops. I was becoming more than a small business owner. I was an entrepreneur!

After I took over the Fullerton shop, I learned the nuances of the location. I also observed the baseline volume, which allowed me to calculate the shop's earning potential. Then, just as before, I went looking for another shop to buy and another family to lease the Fullerton location to. The lease on the Fullerton shop, which was far busier than the La Habra location, went for more money, and I saw how quickly my family's monthly income could accumulate. Once I handed over a shop, I did very little work at that location. I was available to the family for advice, and I arranged shipments from a distributor, but I finished most of my job on the front end.

This was an exciting time for us. I began accumulating shops quickly. I had a knack for scouting locations. I honed the stakeout technique, sitting in my car and observing traffic, taking notes, and sipping coffee. I would watch customers come in and note how long they stayed inside. I was looking for clues that would help me understand how much profit there was to be made. I realized how valuable an existing drive-thru window could be, and I began to see how a shop's position on a block, along with factors like congestion and parking, affected sales. I looked for distinguishing signs and architecture.

Southern California is a dreamland of so-called programmatic architecture. Wide boulevards are lined with shops and restaurants with towering statues holding aloft burgers and ice cream scoops. Some buildings are shaped like the food they serve within—a hot dog, a fudge sundae, and, of course, a donut. These were marketing ploys back in the 1950s and 1960s, when, following World War II, Southern California became the world's most famous car culture. Understanding how people moved through the sprawling, sun-dappled cities was one of the main keys to success in any retail or restaurant business.

There were other skills I picked up. I learned to negotiate options on leases to ensure I wouldn't be kicked out of a location or face steep rent hikes, and I began to make deals with suppliers, lowering my costs by buying in bulk. At each shop, I substituted top quality ingredients and instituted the Winchell's baking schedule of multiple small batches throughout the day. Otherwise, I left things as they were. I also kept the existing names of the donut shops in place. In my opinion, trying to begin a chain of my own had very little appeal, other than perhaps massaging my ego. Nobody would care about Ted Ngoy's donuts. It would be meaningless, and I would have to spend enormous energy on marketing to build up the brand's reputation. But everybody loved their local mom-and-pop shop, and keeping things the same paid off in continued loyalty from longtime customers. With my customers happy, the transition to new ownership was much smoother than it otherwise might have been, and my income grew.

If you had told me years earlier that I would one day become an expert at every facet of the donut business, I might have laughed at you. Early on in my journey to becoming a successful businessman, well-intentioned people advised me to get out of donuts and apply my business talent to a more lucrative industry. But this is a shortsighted way of thinking. Even though the money that could be earned from one shop was small, my expertise allowed me to scale very quickly.

There is an important lesson here for anyone who hopes to become successful in business. Sometimes the greatest opportunities are hiding behind unattractive masks. Say the words "donut shop" to a business school student and they'll conjure images of tired laborers endlessly frying and glazing dough. But success in business is about spotting opportunities without being swayed by image or emotion.

Donuts are high-margin products, and even though a single unit costs less than a dollar, a good portion of that dollar is profit. Margins on coffee are even better. If you can successfully run a high-margin business, then it's a small creative leap to see that you can scale that business and increase your income by leaps and bounds. It doesn't take a genius to understand this, but in the moment of decision, it does require you to see the world through an evaluative and nonjudgmental set of eyes.

How many others saw those ads in the *Register* and scoffed? I can't say everything was planned from the start—like any entrepreneur, I was making a lot of it up as I went along. But I am proud to say that I was humble enough to look at an ad for a donut shop and see opportunity, self-sufficiency, and a better life for my family.

My reputation in the small community of Cambodians living in California began to grow. Everyone had a cousin, a brother, or an in-law who had fled the Khmer Rouge and was having a hard time establishing themselves. If they were willing to work, I could set them up with shops. If no shop was available to buy, I now possessed the knowledge to set one up from scratch. That was my great value-add: the ability to fund shops up front and get them running efficiently. I looked for old fast food locations. Empty Taco Bells were my favorite. They had preexisting drive-thru windows, and typically they were well located. It took far less money to run a donut shop than it did a Taco Bell, which required owners to pay hefty franchise fees, so I could succeed where the name brand restaurant had tried and failed.

By 1979, I had sixteen shops and our fortunes had radically changed. I was collecting between $25,000 and $30,000 per month in lease money. If you had told me just four years earlier that I would be earning more than $300,000 per year in income, I would have laughed. My children had gone from being the sons and daughter of poor immigrants to belonging to a very comfortable family living its own version of the American dream. We moved to a beautiful house in Orange County at the center of our small donut empire. The country that had saved our lives and given us our chance at prosperity now accepted us as citizens. We became quite well known in the Cambodian-American community, and though we were far from millionaires at that time, I was still able to help our friends with gifts of money and loans to start businesses, along with whatever business counsel I could offer.

I distinctly remember the looks on faces of fellow refugees when I gave them seed money to start a little store, to pay off a debt, or to take care of themselves or their families. Money itself has never been particularly appealing to me, though making money would become its own vice in time. But using money to provide for others is a feeling as powerful as any drug.

Immigrant groups take hold in the United States because the country offers all who come so much opportunity. When one family succeeds, it tends to elevate those around it. There weren't too many Cambodians in the United States in 1979, and many of those who escaped in the first wave were well off to begin with. But we were strengthening our ties to our adoptive country, and we were starting to rise as a small immigrant community. Our children were already doing better than we were, making their way through schools and, in the case of older children, entering prestigious universities. Our little enclave gained respect and prestige in the neighborhoods that accepted us. I can't say the phrase enough: It's the American dream.

Little did we know that the number of our countrymen seeking a new life in the United States would soon swell, or that the world would soon have to confront the aftermath of one of the worst atrocities in human history, the same scourge from which my family and so many others in our community had fled.

•••

Toward the end of 1979, news broke: Cambodia was being invaded by Vietnam, and Pol Pot would likely be defeated. By the late 1970s, word of how bad the situation in Cambodia had become was starting to filter out. In the end, not even the most pessimistic observers came close to guessing the levels of the atrocity. Cambodia became a completely closed state during Pol Pot's rule. In the West, there was a lack of interest in intervening in another war in Southeast Asia, so information was scarce. That helps explains how nearly three million Cambodians could be slaughtered during the Khmer Rouge's reign.

The numbers are horrifying, but they don't begin to tell the story of the suffering under Pol Pot. It is a story of death camps and torture prisons, of mass executions and starvation. It is a story of an entire population reduced to the level of farm animals, so that at times those who lived wished they had been killed quickly, as Suganthini's parents were during the invasion in 1975.

The Khmer Rouge had been very successful filling its army with volunteers and forced conscripts from the countryside. The new recruits were largely uneducated and easily manipulated and intimidated. Any hint of dissent was met with violence and death. The entire population of Phnom Penh, about 2.5 million people, was evacuated to the countryside to fulfill the agrarian reforms that Pol Pot preached. Anyone with a higher education was executed outright or purged from the population and sent to one of the prison camps, from which almost no one would emerge. Death was far preferable to conditions in the camps, which were often located in former schools. People were kept in cells so small they couldn't stand, and the methods of torture used by the Khmer Rouge were at once simple and horrifying. Soldiers would tie people's wrists behind their backs and hoist them by their hands until they died. They would chain people up and deny them food and water. They would torture people with crude instruments and extract useless confessions about alleged subversion.

What is rotten must be removed, went a popular Khmer Rouge slogan. Pol Pot bragged that he would create the first society to become totally communist without any intermediary steps, with no easing in. He claimed he was turning the clock back to "year zero." Prisoners, an army of torturers, and the newly dead soon became the capital's only inhabitants. Phnom Penh, the jewel of Cambodia's modern era, was abandoned and left in ruins.

The new agrarian society envisioned by the Khmer Rouge was partly inspired by communist texts, and partly by Pol Pot's admiration for the way tribes in remote areas of Cambodia lived without money, education, or the country's Buddhist religion. Pol Pot wanted all of Cambodia converted to the tribal system, and he enforced his will at the end of his army's guns. The new country, in Pol Pot's mind, would have no social institutions, such as schools, banks, or churches. Modern technology was labeled coercive, an instrument of the capitalist West. The dark ages had returned.

For an isolated society to survive, it must produce all its products internally. Pol Pot set out to triple the country's agricultural production in just one year. Families were forced into agrarian camps and divided into work units. People lived together in crude sheds and spent all day toiling over the land. Each family was given a quota of food it was required to produce. If the quota wasn't met, families were denied sustenance. Thousands died of malnutrition or disease.

Pol Pot failed, of course. You cannot bury a beautiful, sophisticated society like ours and expect to replace it overnight. The downfall officially came at the hands of the Vietnamese, though Cambodia would have starved to death before long if no intervention came. The Khmer Rouge had allied itself with anti-American Vietnamese to come to power. Once Pol Pot seized the capital in 1975, however, the Khmer Rouge leadership feared Vietnam would begin laying the groundwork for an Indochinese federation. Such a federation would be dominated by Vietnam, and that was unacceptable to Pol Pot. As soon as he seized power, he began purging Vietnamese officers and officials from his ranks.

The Khmer Rouge began a protracted war with Vietnam in 1975, attacking a small Vietnamese island and clashing in skirmishes along the border. It was madness. Vietnam's forces vastly outnumbered Cambodia's. Cambodia has always had a small military, and under Pol Pot the fighters faced starvation conditions. Most were poorly trained and they fought out of fear, not faith. In 1977, although there was no chance of victory, the Khmer Rouge mounted a surprise offensive. Vietnam retaliated, and the next years saw more intense fighting along the border, with heavy Cambodian casualties. The Khmer Rouge managed to capture new territory here and there, which raised anxiety levels in Vietnam.

Eventually, tired of the border disputes, Cambodia's neighbor decided to launch an invasion. In late 1978, 150,000 Vietnamese troops invaded Cambodia and overran the capital. After easily seizing control in early 1979, the invading force set up a pro-Vietnamese government, marking the beginning of a ten-year occupation. Pol Pot was forced to flee, but he didn't go quietly. Western Cambodia became a battlefield, and Pol Pot's

Khmer Rouge became a rebel force once again. Millions of land mines were laid, and the border became a death trap for those who would soon try to cross it.

After the fall of the Khmer Rouge, and sensing the smallest window of opportunity, Cambodians began to flee *en masse*. The Khmer Rouge's continuing war with Vietnam, which soon became another proxy in the region, would keep the country in a perpetual state of turmoil for the next decade. After years of starvation, torture, and genocide, Cambodians no longer had any faith in government. With violence erupting along the borders, thousands risked land mines and attack in search of a better life.

•••

In the nearly five years since the Khmer Rouge seized power, my family's fate, as well as the fate of other first-wave Cambodian refugees, had little in common with the fates of our friends and family members back in Cambodia. By 1979, I was making $30,000 per month and living in a beautiful house. Those who managed to flee had only their lives, and they clung to those fiercely. Many died on the journey out. There are countless stories of processions of refugees marching along a trail, only to be met with machine gun fire from Khmer Rouge troops or itchy Vietnamese soldiers.

Visiting one of these men later, I listened in horror as he

recounted how he had stopped to get a sip of water out of a puddle, and then watched as another family, attempting to quench their thirst from the same puddle, stepped in the wrong place and was blown into the sky in a mess of limbs and ripped flesh. These were not combatants, but children and a mother who had survived horrific conditions, only to meet that violent end.

Suganthini and I were heartsick and angered by the stories we heard, and we thought of our families and friends, whom we had not heard from in years. We had found success and forged independent lives, and now we felt we had to do something to help others. I had become well known among the Cambodian-Americans in California, almost like a godfather, and I had a chance to use that prestige to do good. After the Khmer Rouge fled the capital, I contacted the US State Department and asked about sponsoring refugees to come to America. I was told that the refugee crisis was growing by the day and sponsors were needed. After filling out paperwork, we awaited the first family's arrival.

I'll never forget how nervous and hollow-eyed the mother and father looked when I drove to the processing station and picked them up. The children were quiet and fearful, and as they climbed into my car, I had the feeling of being among ghosts. I set the family up in an apartment, gave them money, and took them to the welfare department to get signed up for transitional assistance. When the parents had rested and recovered after their journey, and when they finally felt ready to begin rebuilding, I offered to train them and set them up in the donut business. I have rarely seen more gratitude for such a small gesture. After years of backbreaking labor, the opportunity to work for themselves and create a life for their children seemed miraculous.

The experience solidified my resolve to help my countrymen. I had means and I had the will. Suganthini and I began sponsoring family after family. New Cambodians arrived in Orange County by the dozens, and the community of first-wave refugees did all it could to make them feel welcome. When I ran out of capacity in my donut shops, I looked for more to buy. I had to branch out, moving up the coast to open new territories. Soon I found that the supply of donut shops for sale had dwindled statewide. I was sponsoring a family every two weeks, which meant I couldn't wait for new shops to come up for sale. I had built shops from scratch before, and now I applied myself like a man possessed. I trained many of the refugees myself, installing them in their own shops and taking no money until they got on their feet.

There are certain times in life when meeting an ethical responsibility is also good business. It is a rare and happy intersection. The most precious thing I could offer arriving families was the opportunity to start a new life making donuts. In the process of setting up those shops, my own business expanded. I made far less money on the new refugees than I had on my first leases, but my business grew like wildfire. My family's income tripled in a few short years. By 1985, ten years after arriving in my new homeland penniless, I was netting $100,000 per month. We had surpassed our own wildest expectations, and we had become the embodiment of every immigrant's dream: we were rich.

PART IV
OF VI

MY FALL FROM GRACE CAME AT A MOMENT WHEN SUCCESS FELT FATED and unstoppable. In 1980, I was sponsoring dozens of families from Cambodia, delighting in the thrill that came from helping my countrymen. Money flowed in, and I felt blessed with the positive energy of having earned that money responsibly. My family lived in a comfortable home in La Habra, and my children went to wonderful schools.

After a long time apart, we had reunited with my mother. We sponsored her as soon as we could, and she came to live with us. She had aged significantly during her years living under Pol Pot's brutal regime. Her face was etched with lines of hardship. Fortunately, as a poor woman she was spared the worst violence, which was reserved for anyone belonging to privilege. But to survive she had to farm the land and meet her quotas, and nobody escaped Pol Pot's brutality without deep pain and loss. As she had done when I was a child, she worked hard and survived.

Now that she was with us, my mother slowly began to smile again. She was out of practice after years of living in near-starvation, but her sweet spirit ventured forward, and I watched the glow and kindness return as she sat quietly beside her grandchildren. Call it what you will—a soul, a supernatural grace—but there is an enduring essence in humans, one that all men and women possess, even if they don't know it. It is goodness, and when it is given a chance to breathe free air and be among loved ones, it flourishes.

My mother settled into our happy life. During this period, much of my time was spent mentoring others. Many of the people I trained took my early business education and expanded on their own, opening new donut shops or becoming independent entrepreneurs. It gave me a lot of satisfaction to watch former protégés enrich themselves and their families, and I wore the title "Uncle Ted" with pride.

One of the many young men I mentored was named Ning Yen. Around 1980, I bought a Santa Ana Winchell's shop that had recently closed. I respect Winchell's, the company that gave me my start, but the brand was struggling. It was a time of growth in the fast food industry, and all restaurants were facing stiffer competition. Winchell's locations were costly to run, and many proved unprofitable. I bought the shop for a good price and found a Cambodian family eager to run it.

Soon after the shop opened, I learned that Yen, a soft-spoken young man, had been coming in late at night to learn how to bake donuts from his cousin. When I met him, he seemed to be driven and humble, and I was impressed that he spent his own time without pay in hopes of bettering his life. He reminded me of myself—ambitious, humble, and hardworking—so I gave him a job. To my delight, he became the hardest working employee I had.

Later, Yen shared with me his dream of branching out on his own, and I mentored him along the way. When he asked for help opening his own shop, I gladly cosigned a loan, enabling him to secure a promising location up the coast. He became like part of my family, and eventually he and my nephew set up a distributorship to serve the growing network of Cambodian-owned donut shops. They bought supplies at Price Club and delivered them around Orange County. A few years later, by the late 1980s, the partners moved to a 10,000-square-foot warehouse and began dealing directly with equipment manufacturers and companies like Coca-Cola and Pillsbury.

When business wasn't growing fast enough, Yen borrowed a page from my book and started opening dozens of shops on his own to expand the market for his supplies. There was a brashness to that kind of problem solving, and it allowed many like Yen to find new opportunities overlooked by others and succeed on their own terms. There seemed to be no limit to the forward progress of the Cambodian donut shop owners; often, venturing into a shop, I was rewarded with the kindest smiles and welcomed as a kind of prophet of sweet, glazed success.

Suganthini and I moved into a beautiful house in Mission Viejo. My business was expanding with minimal effort, and I had a lot of time on my hands. That's when two things happened that would throw my life on its head yet again. The first would bring me great joy and accomplishment, and the second would bring me depths of sorrow I did not know existed.

Sensing a need for a bigger Cambodian-American voice in politics, I became active in the Republican Party, a path that would bring me to a position of influence. Around the same time, my wife and I took a trip to Las Vegas to see the shows and take in the sights. I did not gamble on that first trip. We saw a magic act, enjoyed some delicious food, and left. It was such an innocuous beginning to what would become a crippling vice.

•••

There is an image that is seared into my memory. It is a shameful image. I am ducking behind a bank of slot machines. I am in Caesar's Palace, and it is 1987 or '88. The room is full of sound and light—the electronic bells and pyrotechnics of Las Vegas. In a way, that din was reminiscent of our discordant days living in Bangkok, a city whose size and energy made my family uneasy. Only now I felt happy for the distraction. When you are disgusted with yourself, you pray for something more hideous to draw others' attention away.

The atmosphere of Las Vegas allowed me to hide, to drown out my life and what remained of my conscience. I watched my wife from behind the slot machines. Her head swiveled one way, and then another. Our children were by her side. She looked forlorn, the way a person looks when she is desperate and tired. She had probably already searched other casinos. Perhaps she asked the pit bosses if they had seen me. They all knew me, though I doubt they would have told her where I was. I was too valuable to them, a loyal patron. They loved me at Caesars Palace.

Suganthini grasped our children's hands tightly. When she looked in my direction, I ducked back behind the row of slot machines. I waited there, like a convict who ducks away from the spotlight during a jailbreak. When I peered out a few moments later, she and the children had moved on. They hadn't seen me. I was safe—though that was hardly the way anyone else would have described my predicament.

I couldn't let Suganthini see me. She was there to take me home, to beg me to stop gambling and to show me the faces of my children, who missed me. I felt so sorry for her, for all of them, and I hated myself in that moment. It is a powerful image and a haunting memory of my weakness. Most likely it is not a single memory. How many times did it happen? A dozen, at least. My recollection is a collage of many similar moments of shame.

It took five years for me to become addicted to gambling. Or perhaps it took me five years before I began to sense that a deep power surged within me and I recognized the control gambling had over me. For a long time, I believed I could control it. Addiction is funny that way. It acts on you in the sneakiest fashion, assuring you that you are in control, that you can stop any time, and that things have not gotten so bad. The addiction tells you that one roll of the dice, one great hand, is all you need to make things right. Because when things are going well for the addict, life feels so right.

After my first trip to Las Vegas with Suganthini, a trip that was delightful in every way, we made a point to visit that dazzling lighted city often. We were Americans, we were wealthy, and it felt like a rite of passage to enjoy our wealth—not indulgently, but like a couple of happy lovers who no longer needed to worry about the atrocities of a turbulent past or the hardships of an uncertain life. On subsequent trips, I began placing small bets. I was merely curious. Blackjack is so ornamental—the green felt, the colorful chips, the style with which the dealers snap the cards onto the table. I became entranced by the drama of each turn, by the affected emotion in the dealer's voice. I was especially taken by the swells of excitement. It came in little waves at first, like the spikes of a heartbeat on a cardiograph machine. As the cards hit the felt, the spikes peaked. Once all the cards were turned, there was the pause, followed by the rush.

There is nothing like it, a bolt of pure excitement and adrenaline. It is as if the thrill of an entire career as an entrepreneur were condensed into one moment of bliss. I should have been wary right then and there, in those first moments of adulation. Nothing that instantaneously joyful can be of lasting value.

With clarity, and after much meditation, it seems obvious that the same forces that prompted me to take bold risks in business and in love also led me down a path toward compulsive gambling. It is the purest form of risk-taking, the distilled anxiety and thrill behind every business decision and bold declaration of love. I take responsibility for my failings and for each despicable action as a gambler, just as I take responsibility for everything that would soon befall my loved ones and myself.

Nevertheless, to understand what happened, you must understand disease. Compulsive gamblers are afflicted in the same way that alcoholics and drug addicts are. That does not exonerate my actions, but it does help explain them, for there must be some explanation for behavior that is so destructive and illogical.

Soon, my five-dollar bets became fifty-dollar bets. My second year, the sums increased to $100, $200, and even $500. Addicts always need a bigger hit. That is the essence of addiction. It is a game of chase, and the rabbit is always out front, seemingly within reach, but never attainable. In those first years, it didn't seem to matter that the bets were growing. What is $500 to a million-aire? It sounds arrogant, but the sums were trivial to me at that time. I still felt I was playing a game with fake pieces, that I wasn't staking anything real. I certainly had no conception by my second year visiting Las Vegas that I was risking the most valuable things of all: my family, my soul, and my mental well-being.

•••

Between trips to Vegas, my mind was on other things. My business was taking much less of my time, and my gambling was not yet out of control. Politics filled the void. Becoming active in politics seemed a logical outgrowth of my role as a business leader and "uncle" in the Cambodian-American community. Successful immigrant groups in the United States follow similar patterns. First, they find a toehold, then they begin accu-mulating wealth and integrating into society, and finally they become an integral part of their adoptive country, exerting influence over their world and bettering the circumstances of those who follow.

Asians in general had very little voice in local and national politics in the 1980s. Historically marginalized groups like African-Americans had made strides during the 1960s, but Asian-Americans didn't have the same history and hadn't mobilized in the same way. We had very little influence and almost no cultural or political representation in the halls of power. We did have a stake in the issues, though. Cambodians were straddling two worlds. Our friends and family were still in Southeast Asia, so policies surrounding immigration and foreign aid mattered a great deal to us. As businessmen, we also had a stake in securing favorable policies for small business owners.

At first, my involvement with the Republican Party meant little more than making donations. I had plenty of money, and I began donating to congressional races and national campaigns. I would tour the coast, visiting donut shops and local community centers to talk about voters' rights and encourage people to participate in government. I drew crowds for small fundraising events, and my grassroots influence attracted attention from the Republican National Committee. I eventually became prominent enough that local Republican politicians started meeting with me during campaign season. I was an unofficial gatekeeper to a community that was suddenly growing in relevance and economic stature.

It surprised me how little politicians on both sides of the aisle were paying attention to immigrant communities, but I always found I had a receptive audience when I approached Republican leaders. It is a wonderful thing to feel like you are being heard by another person, and though politicians are skillful at acting interested, I was impressed by the thoughtful men and women I met in those early days. They went out of their way to listen to stories and hear the concerns of the Cambodian-Americans I introduced them to, and with that small act of inclusion they secured loyal party members for life.

Here, then, were two visions of Ted Ngoy. One was a successful entrepreneur and family man leading his people toward civic engagement and greater political involvement. This Ted was gaining stature and respect, and for all the world he seemed like the model of the coveted American dream.

And then there was a different Ted, one who coexisted with the first, but who was growing hollower and sneakier every minute. This was the shifty-eyed addict who acted for the benefit of his addiction, a man scarcely recognizable to me. That made it all the scarier once I finally realized that he had me firmly in his clutches.

•••

By 1985, I was making frequent trips to Las Vegas. Without even thinking about it and without formulating a plan, I would get in my car and drive to the airport. Flights left every hour, and it only took forty-five minutes to get to that desert oasis. Minutes after landing, I'd be standing at a high roller table. Gamblers make strange associations, and soon I began to think of Caesars Palace as a second home. In my mind, I even filled it with a colorful cast of friends and extended family members: the dealers, the waitresses, the pit bosses. They were all so eager to join in my enthusiasm, and their happiness made it easy to put down $1,000, $3,000, or even $5,000 bets.

If I won, the chips piled up in front of me. If I lost, it didn't matter—there was plenty more where that came from, and the cost was worth the thrill of the experience. The casinos comped rooms and extravagant meals, and though I never entertained thoughts of unfaithfulness to Suganthini, it was thrilling to be the center of attention in a place full of beautiful women, all of whom were well-trained to pay attention to a man on a hot streak or a rich man down on his luck.

At home, Suganthini began to ask me not to go to Las Vegas. I could see what my trips were doing to her. I was spending less time with my children, and she could feel me slipping away. Among the many things that addiction takes from you, the worst is time. I suddenly had no time for my family. Though I had built a business that needed very little attention to thrive, I could no longer keep up with it. I let lease payments slide, forgot to order supplies, and had no time to acquire more donut shops or expand my income. I became consumed with the thought of getting cash out so I could gamble. When I burned through cash on hand, I began to spend our savings. As quickly as the money came, it began to flow away. It was as if a vampire had descended from the black sky to suck me dry of everything I held dear.

By 1987, I was hiding from my wife in casinos. Her searches became frantic. In truth, I had yet to hit bottom. I still had a lot of money, my wife remained loyal to me in the face of overwhelming proof I was a lost cause, and I hadn't squandered the respect of my community. But I knew I had a serious problem and that my time to pull out of the nosedive was growing short. Summoning my courage, I took a positive step and asked for help. I began attending regular Gamblers Anonymous meetings.

I was amazed at the diversity of the people in attendance. Rich people sat beside people who didn't own more than a single pair of tattered shoes. There were old men and young women, and people of every race and religion. What united us was addiction, along with a burning desire to unburden ourselves of our compulsion. Everyone at the meeting had sad stories. People spoke of losing children to the state, of betting cherished family heirlooms, of spending so much time at poker tables they forgot to bathe or eat and grew weak with exhaustion. The stories would seem incredible to someone who had not grappled with these demons, but the faces that told them, etched with the sorrow of hard lives full of heartache and disappointment, left little doubt they were true.

It was an indescribable relief to discover others who had succumbed to the same curse and were suffering the consequences of their addiction. But it wasn't enough.

Inevitably, I would leave meetings with a fierce commitment never to visit Las Vegas again. Then I would get an idea that I had to test myself. I would board a plane, and the cycle would start again. Like a parasite, the addiction attaches itself to your cleverest faculties and turns those weapons against you to ensure its survival. I remember my mother approaching me with a desperate sternness I had never seen in her. She had lived a long time, had seen much, and was a wise woman.

"Son," she said, "you have so much money. Why do you do this? Why do you have to gamble? What good is more money?"

It was impossible to explain that money had nothing to do with it. I was addicted to a feeling, and money was simply the needle that delivered the toxic dose.

I have noted, over the years, that my willpower is stronger than most men's. But addiction crippled me. I began to grow increasingly fearful of losing everything—my family, my status, and my future. I went to great lengths to keep my addiction secret, fearing the shame of acknowledging my weakness outside of the family and beyond the furtive refuge of my Gambler's Anonymous meetings. But I had to seek help, and so I began making quiet inquiries. Most Cambodians are Buddhist, and so the advice that came back was simple: go to a temple.

I knew a temple in Washington, D.C. I had never been a devout Buddhist, but I believed in powers beyond my own and had great respect for the sacraments of that ancient religion. With hopes of seeking solace and redemption in the arms of the Buddha, I flew to the nation's capital.

It was an ironic place to seek refuge. I had flown there many times as a guest of politicians or to raise money. Those who would have recognized me in D.C. regarded me as a respected spokesperson for a community of growing importance and influence. But I was living in shame, and so I shuffled quickly through the airport and hopped in a taxi. When I arrived at the temple, I breathed deeply and exhaled. The air was crisp and the sun was bright. It was a good day to start over. I went and found the monk in charge, and soon I had replaced my button-down shirt with a robe.

The life of a monk is a simple one. Every effort is made to live in harmony with the outside world. I was not training to become a monk, but I lived as the monks in training did, worked as they worked, and ate as they ate. After a week, there seemed to be a clearing away of temptation, a reordering of what is important in life. I rose early to sweep the temple and meditate alongside my brothers. When my mind drifted, it went to Suganthini and the children. I felt I was achieving clarity—that I was recovering. That was a mistake. As soon as that thought formed in my head, all was lost. An addict never recovers, not truly, and it is a sure bet that the person who tells himself he has overcome his addiction will succumb to it once more.

That is what happened to me. Proud and deeply self-satisfied, I returned to California after a month of simple, purposeful living. My shaved hair grew longer, and my confidence grew right along with it. I became sure of myself—cocky. I made promises to Suganthini, I embraced my children and told them about my new beginning, and I pledged to strengthen the business that had faltered in my absence. And then I went to Las Vegas. I cannot tell you how it is I arrived at the decision to go—I'm sure I conjured some twisted logic—only that the weed planted itself in my mind. Once rooted, there was no way for me to pull it up, so it strangled me. I went to Las Vegas and gambled, and then I went back to Las Vegas. The cycle restarted.

Suspecting the problem might be a matter of dosage, I looked for another temple. I had only stayed at the temple in D.C. for a month. In general, American temples are governed by different philosophies than those found in Southeast Asia. I did some research, and soon I discovered a temple in Thailand near the border with Cambodia. It was not a temple for tourists, nor those wishing for a glancing familiarity with the life of a monk. It was a temple for those utterly devoted to a life of asceticism. It seemed just the thing for a good Cambodian man who had lost his way, and after I contacted the monks in charge, I was given permission to join their order.

Part of me believed that being so close to Cambodia would be good. It was still too dangerous for me to enter the country—the Khmer Rouge hadn't laid down its arms, and internal conflicts were flaring up all over the country—so I got as close to it as I could, disembarking in Thailand and taking a bus to a small Thai village. I had to rebuild myself from the ground up, and what better place to do that than near the land that forged me? There was another reason to go back to Asia: I needed physical distance from my money, from my life in the United States, and especially from Las Vegas. There were other places in the world to gamble, of course, but that city called to me, and the only way to ensure I wouldn't succumb would be to hide many thousands of miles away.

The new temple was nothing like the first temple. My time in D.C. was a vacation compared to the brutal conditions of this new place. We walked barefoot many kilometers over a rock-strewn path. My bloody feet throbbed through the night, and I barely slept. The cold crept into my small chamber and accentuated my hunger. My body changed—I lost the small belly I had developed after so many extravagant Vegas buffets, and my face became gaunt and pale. My cheeks grew hollow, and I started not to recognize myself when I caught my reflection. It was as if all the human features were melting away, leaving only my addiction, that hideous monster.

The three months I spent in the temple were among the hardest of my life, and when I returned to California, I was undeniably a different man. I was emaciated and ashen. My head was shaved and deep ruffles of loose skin had collected under my eyes. I was humbler, spoke more softly, and lived each moment with a new deliberateness.

My wife and children approached me with deference, as if in tribute to the difficulty of my journey and the discoveries made along the way.

But even these changes, as positive as they were, did not go deep enough. I was back in Vegas within weeks of my arrival. Suganthini was forced to hunt for me on the gambling floors, our children at her side. I was hiding from my own family, a disgraced man living out a nightmare. I was like Sisyphus—though unlike Sisyphus, I had condemned myself.

Two things saved me. One, counterintuitively, was my deepening interest in politics. Politics gave me a place to focus my energy, and it gave me a sense of problems bigger than mine, problems that afflicted entire communities, entire countries. Addicts are notoriously self-centered, and the act of looking away went some distance toward relieving my burden.

The other thing that saved me was my conversion to Christianity. I converted at my mother's behest. After my many stumbles, she looked at me with that wise, kind face and told me that I needed to seek a power greater than myself. She had found Jesus after moving to the United States, and she quickly became a prominent member of the Christian community in California. Though nearly all Cambodian immigrants were Buddhist by birth, the diaspora led to a wonderful diversity of religious and cultural beliefs. Christian churches had played an enormous role in the resettlement of Cambodian refugees.

I thought back to Dean, the deacon of Peace Lutheran Church in Tustin, who gave so graciously of his time and who gave my family the critical toehold to begin climbing the American ladder. My first experience in the United States was the experience of kindness at the hands of Christians. They asked for nothing in return and did not pressure me or my family to convert to their religion. In so doing, I believe they planted a seed that began to sprout more than a decade later.

I studied the Christian bible in search of deeper knowledge, and I began attending services. I was promiscuous with churches, hopping from one to another to suck up all the information I could and to receive as many versions of the Christian message as possible. It didn't take me long to feel the powerful presence of something divine, to revel in the excitement of the worshippers at the many services I visited. They praised Jesus in a manner totally foreign to me. A Buddhist's devotion is practiced internally, and the journey is largely private. The Christians I came to know and love let their voices rise to heaven, and the community of worshippers was stronger for it, each man and woman brought closer in the shared experience of praising God.

It is no secret that addicts, in escaping the clutches of their addiction, tend to throw themselves with determination and gusto into new endeavors, pouring the manic energy that sustained the addiction into alternate outlets. It was with that energy and enthusiasm that I began to worship Jesus. Before long, I decided to get baptized. I arranged for preachers from across Orange County to come and help me begin my journey as a faithful Christian. We held the baptism at a lake. One after another they dipped their hands in the water or lowered my head back, and each time I came up feeling at once exhausted and empowered, those contradictory feelings living within me and symbolizing a complicated rebirth.

There are certain moments in my life that feel fated. My memory of these moments is a memory of being guided by forces larger than myself to take extraordinary leaps. One of these moments came with my decision to climb into Suganthini's window and profess my love. Another came when I marched into Winchell's to ask for a position in the management training program. I feel my decision to follow Christ was the most important decision of all, and perhaps the ultimate decision toward which all the others were leading.

•••

With much of my time spent in devotion, I managed to stave off the worst impulses of my gambling addiction. With my remaining time, I began to focus on politics with new vigor. When George H.W. Bush ran for president, I made substantial contributions and helped turn out people from the Cambodian community. As a reward for my efforts, I was invited to attend President Bush's inauguration in 1989, which was a great honor for me. I also began building a large political coalition. The coalition was formalized in 1990 with help from prominent members of the Republican Party, men and women whom I now considered friends.

One of these was Congressman Dana Rohrabacher, a former speechwriter for President Reagan who was elected to Congress to represent Orange County in 1988. Rohrabacher is an amazing man with a large personality. He has been described in the media as a "banjo-playing, folk-singing, arch-conservative surfer," a man who doesn't fit neatly into any mold. Shortly after winning the congressional election, he flew to Afghanistan to join a rebel infantry unit fighting against the Soviets. There was no question that this man would put his life on the line for what he believed, and that left a strong impression on all who knew him.

With help from people like Congressman Rohrabacher, along with boisterous, wonderful people like Congressman Bob Dornan, a former actor turned conservative fire-brand, I became the architect of the Cambodian-American Committee, a coalition that operated under the auspices of the Republican National Convention to raise money to help politicians sympathetic to the Cambodian community win elections. I was named national co-chair for the Asian-Pacific National Republican Coalition, a great honor for me, and a new outlet for my energy. Despite being a relatively small minority, Cambodians began to exert an outsized influence on politics.

In 1991, I helped organize a rally that included Asian-Pacific groups from around the country. The rally was held in Mile Square Park in Santa Ana, and active coalitions representing seventeen Asian-Pacific countries participated. A competition was held to see which group could turn out the most people. Stands went up in the park, elaborate cultural performances were planned, and food from across the region was prepared—tempting bait to attract local attendees. I donated $50,000 to the effort, a portion of which we used to erect a scale replica of the Angkor Wat temple, the most sacred site in Cambodia and the country's primary tourist attraction. Dozens of artists and craftsmen went to work on the model. We advertised heavily, using donut shops as bases of operation to get the word out. The event attracted about sixty thousand participants, and a full fifteen thousand were Cambodian.

Our coalition won two awards from the event organizing committee: one for attracting the biggest crowd, beating out coalitions from Japan, Korea, and India; and one for having the best cultural performance. It was an impressive demonstration, and I received congratulatory phone calls from friends at the National Republican Committee who recognized how vital my efforts were to the future of a country that was being reshaped by immigration and globalization.

Later, I even received an award from President Bush in a ceremony attended by thousands. I proudly stood onstage alongside Asian-American luminaries, including the owner of Toys-R-Us and a prominent general from India. It was one of the proudest moments of my life. Motivated to expand the presence of Cambodian-Americans in politics, I became founder and first chairman of the Cambodian-American Republican Committee, which received official recognition from the RNC. My friends and I were gaining access and influence we never dreamed of in our first years in America.

My involvement in politics was growing at just the time that Cambodia was emerging from its long nightmare. Following the Vietnamese invasion of Cambodia, which drove Pol Pot from power, the country descended into simmering unease. In 1982, the Vietnamese set up a tri-party coalition government consisting of Prince Sihanouk, a non-communist leader named Son Sann, and the Khmer Rouge. Pol Pot had been convicted in absentia of war crimes, but he refused to surrender. His party, which was responsible for the slaughter of three million Cambodians, continued to play a role in the transitional government. Vietnam finally withdrew its forces in 1990, and the various factions entered peace talks in Paris in 1991. Most parties signed a peace accord calling for free elections. Only the Khmer Rouge refused, insisting its members would boycott.

Despite the Khmer Rouge, the country was clearly marching toward a new chapter. An election was scheduled for 1993, to be overseen by the United Nations Transitional Authority in Cambodia. The new government would shape the future of the country. At that time, I had no clear sense of a career in politics, but I was certain that Cambodia would need to ally itself strongly with the United States to enrich its people and avoid further tragedy. Guided by that impulse, I decided to explore the possibility of running for office in the 1993 election. I had not been back to my country for many years, but I felt strongly that my business experience and political connections in the United States could be useful as Cambodia sought to create a new future.

Suganthini was in favor of returning to Cambodia to participate in the elections. "We should do it!" she said enthusiastically, already dreaming of a new start for us in Cambodia. Our relationship had suffered immensely under the strains of my addiction, and though I was keeping my demons at bay thanks to my religion and my grassroots organizing, I could feel the old impulses rising and could imagine how easy it would be to slip back into a spiral of despair. Moving to Cambodia would allow me to continue my political efforts, and it would put important physical distance between me and Las Vegas. And there was an added pressure to act responsibly: if I were running for office, I would be under a microscope and subject to public scrutiny. The fear of losing face and blowing my chances at a role in my country's future would be powerful deterrents against a return to old habits.

Before committing, it was imperative I seek advice and input from my political contacts. Part of the attraction of running for office was to forge a closer alliance between the United States and Cambodia. Stronger economic ties to America meant jobs for Cambodians and a powerful buffer against tyranny. I am a strong believer that global markets can help ensure a more peaceful, prosperous world, and that was the message I hoped to bring to my countrymen.

In search of guidance, I visited my friend Congressman Rohrabacher. The man had fought the Soviets alongside Afghan freedom fighters just a few years earlier, but when I outlined my plan, his face grew dark. He worried that it was unsafe for me in Cambodia and that I risked running afoul of Pol Pot's terrorists, who stalked the jungles and seemed likely to launch an attack ahead of the election. He also worried that I might unintentionally put myself in harm's way by stepping into an uncertain political arena with many competing interests—all this in a country with a recent history of terrible violence. It was not inconceivable that one faction or another would try to intimidate voters or candidates. This was not a decision to be made lightly.

In the end, I told Congressman Rohrabacher that I appreciated his concern, but that I had thought through the dangers and wanted to help my country achieve a more prosperous future. He respected my position and said he'd make some inquiries. He did me a great honor by placing a call to James Baker, the secretary of state and President Reagan's former chief of staff. He asked Secretary Baker for advice and clarification on America's position in the 1993 election. Secretary Baker informed Congressman Rohrabacher that the United States would support the Royal Party of Prince Sihanouk in the election, which meant I would not have any implied backing from Washington. "Do you still want to go?" my friend asked me. I told him I did.

"Well, what can I do to help?" he asked.

If I was going to launch a political party in Cambodia, I needed a name that reflected my political philosophy. "How about something like *development*," Rohrabacher suggested. "Maybe, *free development*."

I told him it sounded good, and it reflected my economic ambitions for Cambodia. But I felt we needed one more element. "You added part of the name, and now I'll add part. What about *Republican*?" I thought for a moment, and then said the name that came to mind: The Free Development Republican Party.

Congressman Rohrabacher smiled. "I like it," he said.

Suganthini and I prepared to return to Cambodia. We spoke to our children, who were old enough to stay behind in the United States. We took out cash, which we would use hiring people on the ground. A strong political apparatus would be imperative. By now, the Cambodian community had many prominent members, and it was easy to divest of the business that had made me wealthy.

It was sad to sell the donut shops, which had been my ticket to success and had brought my family comfort and prestige. But I had a new calling and an important mission.

Before I left, I received a wonderful gift. At the behest of Congressman Rohrabacher and a good friend named John Taylor, the director of the Nixon Library in Yorba Linda, former President Richard Nixon drafted a letter to the Prime Minister Lee Kuan Yew of Singapore. In it, he mentioned me by name and asked for the prime minister's advice. He received a reply encouraging me to stop in Singapore before continuing to Cambodia so that I could receive his Excellency's counsel.

Though Prime Minister Lee Kuan Yew believed it would be better for me to join one of the major political parties than start my own, he nonetheless offered friendly words of encouragement and a wise breakdown of the political situation across the region. It was a great personal honor for me, and a wonderful start to an exciting new chapter in my life: I was setting out to become the leader of a political party to lead Cambodia into the future.

PART V
OF VI

FLYING INTO CAMBODIA FOR THE FIRST TIME IN SEVENTEEN YEARS was deeply humbling. On our approach to Phnom Penh, I looked down at the dense green jungle, which broke onto a quilted patchwork of rice fields. They looked brown and untended in the muggy sun. A deeper hue bloomed along the banks of the Mekong River, which flowed muddy and brown in a slithering arch. At the farthest radius of a long curve, the river gave way to the sprawl of Phnom Penh. Even from the air, it was clear the city had undergone a major transformation. With the passing of time, humans expect advancement, and so it was shocking to see that the city's march had gone in the opposite direction.

Years earlier, I had escaped a modern city that was being chewed into by mortar fire and flooded by an evil of unspeakable magnitude. The city below me seemed anything but modern. It was in ruins, far more decayed than seventeen years could properly account for. It had been destroyed and seemed almost beyond repair. Whole blocks contained little more than rubble. Large buildings stood naked and embarrassed, the neighboring structures bombed away. Vines and vegetation choked abandoned houses. I felt a pang in my heart when I touched down on the bumpy airstrip, and I squeezed Suganthini's hand. She smiled, but I could tell her outward strength concealed depths of emotion.

According to the new constitution, the government of Cambodia would be a parliamentary democracy. Political parties would vie for seats, and the party with the majority would nominate a prime minister. My hesitation to throw my lot in with the major parties had to do with influence. The newly formed parties were run by men who had clear visions for Cambodia backed by strong ideologies formed in the crucible of civil war. I respected many of these men, but I also knew they would not tolerate voices of dissent from within the ranks of their parties. I had my own beliefs about governance, and I'd formed nearly all of them through my experience in American politics.

No politician can say he is entirely selfless, and like all candidates, I was romanced by the thought of a public career. But to a larger degree, I entered politics with the mind of a businessman. I didn't have an ideology, only experience. My agenda was not based on an adherence to a strong political philosophy—I was not a communist and not a royalist, which were the dominant strains in Cambodian politics. For that reason, I concluded that I would not be well represented by the two major parties that had formed seemingly overnight.

I wanted to rejuvenate my country through smart economic development initiatives and an American-style emphasis on freedom. To do that, I needed a strong independent voice. I would start my own party, and I would barnstorm the country to win votes. At best, I hoped to capture a seat or two in the legislature.

It was easy to dream of mobilizing my countrymen, but it proved difficult to create a political apparatus and run a successful campaign in a country that had almost no infrastructure. Suganthini and I rented a villa in Phnom Penh. It was December 1992 when we arrived, and we had just six months to register our party and begin whipping votes. I invited several prominent businessmen to join the new party, and I began hiring Cambodians sympathetic to our cause to help spread the word. Our enthusiasm was high, but we immediately ran into obstacles.

In the United States, politicians raise money so they can spread their message in the media. In fact, the US system of democracy would not work without a strong, independent media, which is why the press is called the Fourth Estate. But most Cambodians didn't have televisions or radios at that time. After years of torment under the strict and murderous Khmer Rouge regime, the notion of reading a newspaper or asking informed questions to arrive at an independent opinion was completely foreign to most Cambodians.

Add to this the fact that Cambodians were deeply suspicious of anybody seeking power in the new government. It was the government, after all, that had orchestrated the slaughter of three million and the torture of so many more. The fear was completely justifiable. For all anybody knew, the new elections would put another strongman in place, and everybody feared being punished in the future if they voted for the wrong candidate. Everywhere I went, I saw fear in the eyes of my countrymen, and I felt incapable of breaking through with a message of hope.

Compounding matters, I was an outsider. Though I had been born poor in the Cambodian countryside, my wealth and my status as a Cambodian-American made me a different species in the eyes of the people whose votes I needed. Though we shared the same roots, we did not share the same recent history.

The campaign plodded along achingly slowly. My hired team spread out over the country arranging speaking opportunities at schools and pagodas. In hindsight, the campaign was unfocused and too geographically dispersed. When I showed up to share my message of economic development and world trade, I often found myself talking to an audience of no more than a handful of farmers.

I was happy to be connecting with real people, but with little time before the election it was difficult to imagine our ground game winning enough hearts and minds to gain a seat in the legislature. By my estimation, the party would need at least forty thousand votes to win a seat. My people hired cars and drove around blaring campaign slogans. We printed leaflets and passed them out *en masse*. But the tactics seemed to get us nowhere.

As if we needed more challenges, we were constantly working under threat. There was very little security in Cambodia at the time, and everywhere we went we felt watched. Saying the wrong thing or upsetting the wrong people could result in quick violence, and we heard reports all over the country of skirmishes and attacks. We never went out at night. There were rumors of secret police hired by powerful men with political ambitions. The situation was so volatile and chaotic that it was easy to imagine the murder of a would-be politician might pass without much of a ripple.

We pressed on, suppressing our fear as best we could, and I met many wonderful people on the campaign trail—men and women who wanted a better future for the nation. Cambodia was no longer under the control of Pol Pot, but it was clear that my people still felt isolated, in danger, and skeptical of those who wished to help. Their faces looked as if they had walked through hell.

One month before the election, I invited Congressman Dana Rohrabacher to visit the country. He and a cadre of six support personnel flew into Phnom Penh to tour the area. It was a privilege showing the congressman my country, where the fragile roots of democracy were just beginning to take hold. No matter what happened during the election, I knew Cambodia's future depended in large part upon establishing a close relationship with the United States. The congressman's visit, and his optimistic outlook toward a country in the throes of rebirth, gave me hope that Cambodia would flourish under the tutelage of the world's greatest democracy.

Twenty political parties were competing in the election, and during his visit, Congressman Rohrabacher invited representatives from all twenty parties to a meeting. His message was clear: Cambodia needed democracy and the rule of law. He illustrated the point with a beautiful metaphor. Holding his hand out, he said the destiny of Cambodia is like a bird you hold in your hand. If you squeeze the bird, it will die. But if you release the bird and let events take a natural course, it will flourish. Back in the United States, the congressman's colleagues hoped Cambodia's politicians would allow democracy to take its course.

•••

In May 1993, to everyone's relief, the elections proceeded largely without incident. But when the tallies came back, we learned we had not won a seat. Our efforts had not been wasted—we gathered approximately twenty thousand votes, which was a minor miracle given the constraints and short timeframe of our campaign. But it was a humbling defeat, and a lesson that money and passion, though a powerful mixture, are sometimes not enough. I thanked my staff, congratulated them on a hard fight, and assured them that their efforts had made a difference. Then I dismissed them, and Suganthini and I found ourselves alone for the first time in months.

The election did have a silver lining for me. Though I had not won a seat in the new government, the campaign attracted the attention of powerful people. My reputation continued to grow following the election, thanks to my role in the Cambodian community in the United States. As expatriates slowly began returning to Cambodia, stories of the "Donut King" filtered through society, and soon I had a surprising invitation.

The royalist party led by Prince Sihanouk's son, Norodom Ranariddh, had won most seats in congress, so Prince Ranariddh was named first prime minister. But the royalist party formed a coalition government with the Cambodian People's Party (CPP), which won the second-most seats, and in hopes of unifying the country, the parties agreed to the unusual solution of appointing two prime ministers. Prince Ranariddh would be first prime minister, and the head of the CPP, an intelligent man named Hun Sen, would be second prime minister. About eight months following the results of the election, I was approached by the special envoy from both prime ministers, a man named Nhim Vanda. He informed me that

Second Prime Minister Hun Sen wanted to meet. A date was set and I arrived at Hun Sen's residence, a humble dwelling near Independence Monument. The second prime minister greeted me with a smile—he projected warmth and expressed an interest in my experience as an expatriate returning to Cambodia. I congratulated him on his party's performance in the election, and we began speaking honestly about the future of the country and the challenges Cambodians would face in their climb toward self-determination.

"What do you plan to do with yourself, brother, now that the election is over?" he asked me.

I told him I was considering going back to the United States. He looked me in the eyes, and I will never forget his reply.

"Please don't go back, Brother Ngoy. There is so much we can do together if you stay."

Hun Sen had heard about my business acumen and saw in me a tool he could use to help rebuild the country. He asked my thoughts on the economy. I had spent many months touring and talking about my plans, so my answer was clear and concise. I told the second prime minister that economic development was imperative and we needed to attract interest from foreign businesses to secure well-paying jobs for our citizens. We talked a little longer, and I shared an idea with him. Humbly, I suggested he oversee the creation of a chamber of commerce.

He was not familiar with that sort of institution, which is a Western innovation, and asked for clarification. I explained the French version of a chamber of commerce, which is a semipublic and semiprivate entity, and the English and American version, which is fully private. The point of the institution, I said, is to give industry a forum to speak with public officials and easily access resources and information to do business. I told him it was fundamental that Cambodia become an easy, attractive place for foreign entities to trade and set up factories.

Hun Sen liked the idea. He summoned Nhim Vanda and ordered him to speak with the Minister of Commerce, a sharp man named Var Huot Who. The second prime minister wanted to make me the first president of the new chamber, but he could not make the decision unilaterally. Var Huot Who approved of my appointment, and I soon received word from Excellency Sok An, a senior minister on the council of ministers, that the arrangements would be made official following the return of a Cambodian economic delegation to Japan. Hun Sen, who had traveled to Japan with the envoy, instructed me through the minister to begin looking for foreign investors. In my mind, as well as the minds of those people closely involved with the decision, the appointment was as good as made—or so we thought.

When the letter crossed the desk of the first prime minister, Prince Ranariddh, the plans came to a screeching halt. The first prime minister liked the idea of a chamber of commerce well enough, but he refused to sign off on my appointment as president. I believe in the prince's eyes I was a political opponent. In the context of Asian politics, republicans are seen in opposition to royalty and in favor of a weaker central government. The prince balked at the idea of instating me as an important appointee, fearing that I would be another opponent he would have to keep his eyes on.

I wished to help lead the nation, and the lack of an appointment to the chamber was discouraging. Still, I vowed to help get the institution operational and lend counsel however I could. The chamber opened in 1995, giving foreign investors a direct line to the government and a much simpler way to pursue opportunities in Cambodia. The same year, Hun Sen appointed me as his advisor on economic affairs, a great honor, and one that finally gave me an official seat at the table.

•••

In 1995, there was not a single factory in Cambodia that made goods for export. Our people had no education and few marketable skills. A pessimist might look at the situation and despair. But a student of history didn't have to look far to find an encouraging corollary. In the middle of the twentieth century, Taiwan was in pitiful shape. Children walked around without shoes, and the tiny nation-state had no appreciable export economy. By the 1990s, however, Taiwan was considered the dragon of Asia, exporting all kinds of goods to the United States and Europe.

The shift occurred when Taiwan received an all-important designation from the United States, becoming a "most favored nation." Getting MFN status guaranteed Taiwan favorable tariffs for its exports to the United States, which opened a vast new market. Just as important, it signaled to companies and investors all over the world that the United States, the most powerful economy on earth, had faith in Taiwan's future and its commitment to uphold trade agreements. Soon after gaining MFN status from the United States, Taiwan received a flood of international investment. Speculators bought up vast swaths of land and sold parcels to factory owners. Companies in search of cheap manufacturing gave lucrative contracts to the new factories. An entire generation received jobs.

The success of Taiwan's manufacturing sector eventually led to the growth of other sectors and the arrival of a strong education infrastructure, better government welfare programs, and a much-improved standard of living. The entire transformation could be traced to the granting of MFN status by the United States. That gave me a bold idea.

Among my contacts, I was in touch with Ron Abney, the director of operations for the Cambodia office of the International Republican Institute. The American non-partisan organization had a mandate to promote democracy around the world, and Abney was an ardent supporter of Cambodia's move toward a multiparty democracy and an open market economy. I had been thinking privately about the idea of lobbying the United States for MFN status for Cambodia. In 1995, as newly minted advisor to Second Prime Minister Hun Sen, I approached Abney, whom I had first met during the campaign.

"Ron, I'm thinking of doing something very important for Cambodia," I told him.

Abney considered himself a freedom fighter, and he was well connected in Washington. He leaned forward, eager to hear my idea. It was simple, really: if we could secure MFN status for Cambodia, the medium- and long-term economic benefits would be consequential. He considered this for a moment.

"Ted," he said, "give me three days. I'm going to make some calls."

Abney set to work taking the temperature of his colleagues in Washington. Three days later, true to his word, he called me with news.

"Ted, we can do it. We have backing."

Abney had spoken to his contacts, and there was agreement that although it wouldn't be easy, an energetic lobbying effort on the part of Cambodia would likely be enough to tip the scales. The next step was to solicit backing from Cambodia's leadership. I approached Hun

Sen and explained what I wanted to do. He listened with interest, but when I had finished speaking he waved his hands.

"You can try it," he said, "but you'll never get the MFN."

He was under the impression that the American government had already denied Cambodia MFN status. His confusion stemmed from a misunderstanding about the American system of governance. It was true that the issue had been brought up in Congress without satisfactory resolution. In fact, the House of Representatives had already approved Cambodia's MFN status, but the Senate had failed to take up the issue. Without any movement, most officials in Cambodia believed the proposal had languished and expired. But if we could get the Senate to bring the matter to a vote, the issue had a chance of passing.

I explained that the best option would be to lobby Washington, and I asked for permission to proceed. With Abney's support, I was convinced our goal was achievable, and I told Hun Sen I would use my own resources to pursue it. It seemed a small sacrifice in service to a greater goal. He gave me permission, and I reported back to Abney: we were in business.

It is exhilarating to have an ambitious objective, and I have always enjoyed figuring out how to fit the pieces of a puzzle together to achieve some difficult goal. With Abney's support, I approached my political contacts, including Representatives Bob Dolan, Dana Rohrabacher, and Ed Royce. I also approached Senator John McCain of Arizona, whom I had met during my years as a West Coast fundraiser for Republicans. McCain, a Vietnam War veteran, had a special interest in Southeast Asian affairs, and he was a staunch supporter of opening markets in countries like Cambodia. Through my contacts, I received an introduction to Senator William Roth of Delaware, chairman of the Senate Ways and Means Committee, who was sympathetic to our objective. Roth and his team of aides threw their support behind the project and offered to help us in any way they could. He even allowed me to work out of the office of his chief of staff.

A window in the office overlooked the Senate floor, and whenever the body was in session I had an unobstructed view of the men and women engaged in the day-to-day business of running the United States. I also had a clear view of the individuals I would need to win over to secure a better economic future for my country. My job was to lobby Washington, making the case for Cambodia and convincing senators who had only negative associations that the quickest possible way toward stability and peace was through open market strategies.

The large office overlooking the Senate floor became my war room. With the help of Roth's chief of staff, I created a list of senators whose votes we'd need. I wrote the names on a big strategy board in the office, and I began my campaign. Lobbying is an art of persistence, flattery, and negotiation. It's also an art that must be performed in person. I began flying regularly between Cambodia and Washington, D.C., and for several months I lived my life entirely out of suitcases. I wrote dozens of letters to senators and spent long hours on the phone with aides, laying out my case and slowly working my way into meetings with elected officials.

I encountered the most opposition from Democrats, which is not surprising given that my circle of supporters were all Republicans. Democrats seemed unconvinced that Cambodia had turned a corner. One particularly galling charge was that Hun Sen constituted another brutal dictator, that he had blood on his hands, and that he would soon be responsible for the killing and suppression of many Cambodians if left unchecked. This belief stemmed from a misunderstanding about Cambodia's recent history. Hun Sen was, in fact, a member of the Khmer Rouge during the genocide, but so were many tens of thousands of decent Cambodians. It was safer to join the party, even nominally, than it was to be outside of it and subject to victimization.

Years later, when the United States invaded Iraq, the Bush administration made the same error in judgment that these Democratic senators were making when they disallowed any member of Saddam Hussein's Ba'ath Party from participating in the new government. Since virtually everyone in the country with administrative experience had been forced by circumstance to pledge allegiance to Hussein, Iraq was left without any representatives capable of leading the complex transition once the Americans were ready to hand over power. It is, of course, crucial that people be held to account for past sins. But it's also crucial that we look at the facts of history and not rush to judgment based on preconceived notions.

To the charges that officials in Cambodia's new government were corrupt or violent, I offered a simple response, which I repeated so often I still remember it verbatim:

I have come to Washington, D.C., and I have come to you. I am not asking you for power. I am not asking you to support any single person or party in Cambodia. And I am not asking for weapons. I am simply asking for you to give opportunity to millions of people who have had no opportunities for more than a generation. By granting Cambodia the status of Most Favored Nation, our American friends can give us food, jobs, and prosperity. If you have another idea for bringing those fundamental needs to Cambodia, then please tell me. Otherwise, I humbly ask that you support us in this critical time. Cambodia has suffered long enough, and we do not need another prolonged punishment.

This always quieted down the critics. It was no secret in the chambers of power in Washington, D.C., that the atrocity of three million slain Cambodians lay not solely on the shoulders of Pol Pot, an evil and ruthless tyrant, but also on the shoulders of the most powerful country on earth. The United States could have intervened but in the wake of the Vietnam War, it chose to withdraw from the region entirely. Privately, many representatives of the American government felt a great sense of shame at the nation's failure to act, and respectfully reminding them of that failure proved to be an effective strategy.

Over the course of a year, I spent tens of thousands of dollars on travel, hotels, meals with politicians and aides, and the various expenses involved in trying to convince some of the most powerful people on the planet to take me seriously. We made great strides, and after several months we believed we had enough votes. But just when we thought the vote would proceed, Senator Roth's chief of staff called me with some troubling news. One of the committee members, Senator Bill Graham, was holding out. We scrambled to figure out what he wanted. It turned out he would vote in favor of MFN status only if he could secure a favorable trade deal concerning Mexico and the import of tomatoes. It was a lesson in how arbitrary politics can sometimes be. Senator Roth worked on our behalf, and eventually a compromise was reached. Shortly after, I received a phone call.

"Ted," said Senator Roth's chief of staff, "I have good news. We got it. We got the MFN."

After so much effort, I was overjoyed. I cried for several hours. Then I made my official report to General Pel Nal, a close assistant to Hun Sun to whom I reported throughout my effort. My next order of business was a press conference. Standing in front of reporters, I announced that, thanks to the wisdom and bravery of the US Senate, my country's future would be more prosperous, more secure, and more peaceful.

•••

It was a time for celebration. The Cambodian minister of commerce, Cham Prasidh, flew to the United States and we met with Var Huot, Cambodia's ambassador to Washington. The group began making the rounds to thank the senators and congressmen who had been instrumental in our effort. We had dozens of lunches and coffee meetings, but the ambassador had trouble reaching Senator McCain's office to arrange a meeting for the minister of commerce to offer his thanks. He requested my assistance, and Senator McCain's chief of staff came to the phone when I called.

"Ted," he said, "I thought you had returned to Cambodia by now."

I explained that we were trying to reach the senator so the minister of commerce could thank him in person for his help. Senator McCain's support had been very important to our effort. He understandably took a hard line against Southeast Asian regimes. His backing of the MFN was a strong signal to other senators that this was the correct move, one that would help secure peace for a region long troubled by violence.

"Of course, Ted. What time do you want to do it?"

"How about ten o'clock in the morning?"

"Great, I'll clear some space on the senator's calendar."

The next day we met Senator McCain at his office. He was very formal with the ambassador and the minister of commerce. But when he shook my hand, he used one of his fingers to scratch the inside of my palm. "My friend, Ted, how are you?" He asked, speaking slowly and providing me with the private recognition of a shared moment. We had worked closely together to get the MFN passed, and I feel honored to have been considered a friend by so great a man.

Back in Cambodia, the significance of our accomplishment was beginning to sink in. I was summoned by the king, Prince Sihanouk, who congratulated me on my efforts, going so far as to say I had acted heroically on Cambodia's behalf. The Second Prime Minister was also overjoyed, and we toasted Cambodia's good fortune over dinner. During my lobbying effort, China was also actively lobbying the US Congress for MFN status. The Chinese spent millions of dollars and engaged a law firm in support of their effort. At the end of all of that, China was able to procure MFN status only for a single year with a strict trade quota, an arrangement subject to US renewal each year. Cambodia's MFN status was granted permanently and without condition, a testament to what a few dedicated people can do if they apply themselves fully.

Cambodia's MFN went into effect in 1996. Foreign business leaders had been following our efforts closely, and they began approaching the chamber of commerce daily. Though I had not been appointed president of the chamber, I was deeply involved in the organization, and I felt a personal responsibility for its success. I met dozens of manufacturers, and I facilitated introductions with investors who had been purchasing large swaths of land and erecting warehouses and factories. The pace of the development in the manufacturing sector surpassed even my grandest expectations. It was an exciting time, and all of us who worked for the benefit of Cambodia felt we were finally taking important steps out of a long period of darkness.

Businesses from Japan, Korea, and Australia established footholds in Cambodia, and they were soon followed by businesses from China and Taiwan, and then Singapore and Thailand. It was an odd sight, at first, to see wealthy people driving luxurious cars down the ramshackle boulevards of Phnom Penh. But soon foreigners became a common sight in the capital, and it wasn't unusual to go out to a nice restaurant and hear a beautiful cacophony of languages.

Shortly after Cambodia received MFN status, my friend Ron Abney approached me. He had been asked by Washington to secure a direct line of communication and influence with Cambodia's government to ensure that the trade goals of the two countries continued to evolve in lockstep. To that end, Abney asked me to secure a more prominent role as an advisor on economic affairs to the royal government. Considering we owed the American people a tremendous debt, I didn't believe the request would meet any resistance, and I signaled as much to Abney. Hun Sen supported expanding my role, but once again, when the request reached further into the government, I was stonewalled. Politics is a delicate business, and because I was not in the royal family's inner circle, I was still regarded with suspicion. To my great embarrassment, I was unable to honor the request from Washington. I personally lobbied the government to give some sign of thanks to the Americans, but I got no traction.

Understandably, Ron Abney was very upset. He had called in many personal favors and put his reputation on the line to help Cambodia secure MFN status. When he and Washington asked for a small favor in return, they were ignored. Years later, I saw Abney on the street and waved. He turned his back. I have relived that moment many times, and I have shed many tears late at night. It is my sincerest hope that my friends in Washington understand how deeply sorry I am that Cambodia did not hold up its end of the bargain in those delicate early months. In the long run, of course, Cambodia and the United States have forged a close bond, and I strongly believe the granting of MFN status acted as glue holding our nations together.

After the embarrassment of not being appointed as an advisor, I felt I had to do something to show Cambodia's appreciation. I decided to organize a rally to thank the United States for its kindness and express a sentiment of fraternity and appreciation. The rally would be held in the National Stadium, which is so central to life in Phnom Penh. I used my own money to rent the stadium, and I began to go from factory to factory to ask the managers to please allow their workers to participate and thank the nation that helped Cambodia secure greater economic stability. It was not difficult to convince the people who had benefited from the MFN to throw their weight into a show of thanks and appreciation, and soon we had the makings of a large event.

In my haste, I forgot to procure official approval prior to the ceremony, which is important in a country that functions largely on rules of decorum. To my great relief, Hun Sen sent word through an assistant named Ith Sam Heng (now minister of labor) just hours before the event was scheduled to begin: *I wish you success for this morning's festivities.* The American flag rose over the National Stadium, marking a historic first. The stadium was crammed to capacity, and the best estimates were that fifty thousand people showed up to celebrate, making it the largest pro-United States event in the history of Cambodia.

Speeches were made, television crews broadcast the festivities, and journalists helped spread the word back to the United States that the people of Cambodia were grateful. Given the long communist history of our country and the tensions between the West and Southeast Asia, the rally was an important moment of public thanksgiving and a successful demonstration of Cambodia's eagerness to cooperate with the United States.

•••

Before coming to Cambodia, gambling had decimated my fortune. In my bid to win a seat in the legislature, I spent a great deal of my savings. The campaign to secure MFN status had not been cheap, and when I looked at my finances closely, I was forced to accept a new reality. I still had more money than most, but Suganthini and I were no longer wealthy.

Money is a funny thing. Impossible though it seems, the person who has $20 million is often more likely to lose the shirt off his back than the person who works diligently for $20,000 a year. Part of becoming rich is having the ability to think on a different scale than others. Those who risk little and aim low may lead comfortable lives, but it is very unlikely they will become wealthy. On the other hand, those who take big risks and believe they will achieve great things sometimes succeed.

I have never been afraid to invest in myself and my dreams, and that has brought me what others sometimes mistake for incredible luck. But I have also been on the losing end of risk. With the MFN secured and my finances dwindling, I knew each risk I took carried the possibility of financial ruin. I took the risks anyway, and I would live with the consequences.

The next election would be held in 1998, and again I decided to throw my hat in the ring. I yearned for a larger voice in the governance of my country, and I believed I had demonstrated my leadership and vision by helping to secure an economic future for Cambodia. I became a man obsessed. I held political rallies and traveled with members of my team to distant provinces. We were far more organized than the first election, I toured the countryside and spoke until my throat was hoarse.

But the campaign faltered. Cambodia's strong recovery, which occurred in large part thanks to new development and foreign investment, had attracted many wealthy people who wanted to play a role in politics. Competition was fierce, and I was being outspent by the large parties. I again considered joining one of the existing parties, but I couldn't bear the thought of having to fall in line behind leaders I did not fully agree with. I operate best by instinct, not by platform.

Suganthini and I worked hard, as did the staffers who made up the campaign. But when the dust settled, we had again failed to capture a seat. It was a discouraging defeat, and a costly one. I was left with $450,000 in the bank—a fraction of my former fortune. Once again, I felt like a man in need of a big break.

PART VI
OF VI

IF HARDSHIP CREATES CHARACTER, THEN I HAVE MORE CHARACTER than most. I have known periods of great difficulty in my life, but the years between 1999 and 2009 were more trying than I could have imagined. During a turbulent decade, I lost everything.

It began when Suganthini decided to leave Cambodia and travel back to California. Our son, Chris, was expecting his second child, and she wanted to be on hand when Chris's beautiful wife, Staling, gave birth. Suganthini loved being a grandmother, and her decision to return to California made sense. I weighed returning as well, but I elected to stay. I saw tremendous opportunity for financial success in the country's emerging economy.

Suganthini and I talked about it for a long time, and we came to a painful decision, agreeing it would be best if she returned to California indefinitely while I stayed in Cambodia to pursue new business ventures. We would miss each other terribly, but we had been through so much in the last years; a temporary parting of ways seemed like a small bump on the long road of destiny.

I accompanied my wife to the airport and watched as she walked down the jet bridge to the plane. Before I lost sight of her, she turned back and waved. If I had known then it would be the last time we would look at each other as husband and wife, as two people with a future together, I would have called out, would have run after her, and would have flown back to California alongside the woman I loved. But we can't know how life will turn out, and in the moment my decision seemed clear. I had unfinished business in Cambodia, and California still carried associations of addiction and weakness. It was not time for me to go back.

Following the election in 1998, I had about $450,000 to my name. That was still a substantial sum in Cambodia, but not enough, perhaps, to effect change on a massive scale. After seeing the influence that MFN status was having on our economy, I felt more driven than ever to become a leader in Cambodia's recovery. As in the elections, pride motivated me to some extent, of course. But all men who have done great things have a measure of pride. I believed that I could pursue prosperity while also helping my fellow man. I had done it in California, becoming a millionaire while simultaneously helping others pull themselves into self-sufficiency, and I believed that with the right idea, the right connections, and a lot of hard work, I could accomplish something similar in Cambodia.

I had been denied a position as the head of the Chamber of Commerce, but the chamber's incoming president recognized that I could be valuable. In part, this was due to my background doing business abroad, and in part it was due to my language acumen. The new president of the chamber spoke Vietnamese and Khmer, to which I added English, Chinese, and French, important languages in international affairs. Upon his election, the man appointed me as his personal representative.

In addition, I was named head of the chamber's agricultural sector and head of international corporate relationships. The work was satisfying, and in my new capacity I met many men and women who were making incredible contributions in a variety of sectors, and especially agriculture. Perhaps none impressed me more than the Chinese scientists who were revolutionizing farming through hybridization.

Because of its enormous population, which had already exceeded one billion people, China was leading the charge to maximize food production through scientific advancement. Using selective hybridization methods, scientists had created new high-yield varieties of rice. In Cambodia, poor farmers made up about 85 percent of the agricultural sector. Using conventional methods, these farmers were lucky to harvest three tons of rice from one hectare of fertile land. But in China, the same area could produce twelve or even fifteen tons. The Chinese had pulled off what many were calling a miracle.

I had read about hybridized rice in the news—it was a popular story in the late 1990s—and soon had a chance to meet the scientists behind the breakthrough. Regrettably, those first meetings were awkward and tense. A Chinese delegation came to Cambodia to promote the latest agricultural technology. The delegation included about thirty members of the Chinese government and representatives from the agricultural sector, most of them from the provinces of Yunnan and Hunan, which were leading the country in rice yields. Among the visitors were the governor of Yunnan province and the chairman of Yunnan's chamber of commerce.

It was an economic goodwill mission, not an official state visit, but the delegates were expecting an audience with Prime Minister Hun Sen. On a previous visit to China, Hun Sen had personally invited the scientists to Cambodia. Unfortunately, word of the delegation's arrival did not get to the prime minister. It was the kind of simple error that can happen in an emerging democracy when the mechanisms of diplomatic communication are still being worked out. Oversight or not, the Chinese felt insulted, and a volatile situation soon erupted.

I spoke Chinese, and I was also in charge of agricultural affairs for the chamber, so I was doing most of the talking during the meeting. I could tell members of the Chinese delegation were upset by what they perceived to be a deliberate insult. I defused the tension as best I could. When the meeting ended, I asked the head of the delegation if I could visit them at their hotel later that evening to talk about their problems. When I arrived, I found the entire delegation waiting for me in the lobby. Members of the group stood up and treated me with respect, but again they asked why the prime minister had not come to greet them. That's when I lost my temper. I pride myself on my restraint, but my face turned beet red as I lashed out.

"You are all representatives of the Chinese Communist Party, correct?" I asked them. "What, may I ask, is the goal of the Communist Party? I thought it was to help the poor. But you have come all this way to share a technology that can help the poor, and all you are worried about is a proper reception from the prime minister? It doesn't sound to me like you want to help the poor at all!"

When I finished, everyone looked at me in stunned silence. I was surprised myself. Asian business is conducted according to nuanced rules of formality, and it is very rare to see someone lose their temper in a meeting. The Chinese delegates were certainly not accustomed to being spoken to in that fashion. Fortunately, I saw at once that they were embarrassed by their behavior and felt ashamed after being reprimanded. All at once they began treating me like the most important man in the country.

"Excellency," the head of the delegation said, using an honorific that is common in Asia, "why don't you come visit Yunnan province? We want to show you our high-yield rice. If you come, you will be amazed, and the rice may help the people in your country."

I calmed down. I was flattered by their invitation and optimistic about the prospect of bringing hybridized rice to my countrymen. I agreed to visit China and see the miracle for myself. Prior to the trip, I made a point of reading more about the emerging science. I soon became obsessed with the technology and convinced that it may in fact be a powerful tool for fighting hunger and poverty and alleviating the constant fear of drought and famine. Cambodia was so fragile at that time, and a disruption in the agricultural sector could be devastating. China's hybridized rice could act as a kind of insurance policy against such a disruption.

I also saw a financial opportunity. The new rice, which did not reproduce on its own, would have to be imported from China every season. Though the seed would be inexpensive for farmers, there was a large market for it, so the potential profits were huge. This was exactly the sort of business opportunity I was looking for—I could help my country leap away from the jaws of hunger and poverty, and I could make a nice profit on the side. Before the trip, I started an umbrella organization through which I could begin a hybridized rice testbed in Cambodia. I called it the Federation for Advanced Agricultural Development.

•••

The Chinese paid my way to Yunnan province, and I was accompanied on the trip by a Chinese friend and former journalist who had business dealings in Cambodia. The man's name was Wang Yan Yu. For years he was a noted journalist in China, but he had bravely sacrificed a promising career to pursue business on his own in Cambodia, which at the time was the Chinese equivalent of the Wild West. He was a bright man, although he had not yet struck it rich, and I was happy to help him by offering a place to live in those years. Something told me that this man was special and that our fates were entwined—and indeed, that would later prove to be the case.

We drove in a long procession out to the quilted green paddies dotting the countryside. Rice farms are beautiful, and watching the farmers work the flooded fields is like taking a trip to an ancestral time when those methods were first developed. But if farming rice is an ancient technique, these fields were like nothing we had seen before. The miracle I had read so much about was even more impressive in person. In Hunan, we found fields that seemed to explode with life. It was as if the soil on each field came straight from Eden and was blessed with a supernatural fecundity. We visited several agricultural sites and met the scientists, farmers, and government officials overseeing each. I listened to the stories of farmers who had previously struggled year after year to produce enough rice to support their families. Now they were enjoying bumper crops each season. Gratitude to the scientists beamed from watery eyes as they told their stories.

One of the head scientists was Li Jing Yao, a father of hybridized rice in China. Scientists like him were heroes, and as we spoke, I could see why. Li Jing Yao explained that he had always wanted to help the poor. Rather than do so through politics, he found a way with science. As we drove away from the happy farmers and their bursting green paddies, Li Jing Yao confided that he had a tender spot for Cambodia in his heart. He said it was a dream of his to help the Cambodian people, who had suffered so greatly in recent memory.

When the trip concluded, I had a large file of research and dozens of contacts. I also had a grand vision: I was committed to bringing China's agricultural bounty to Cambodia. But it wouldn't be as easy as it sounded. Hybridized rice is bred to succeed in specific areas under very specific conditions. The fields we saw overflowing with vegetation in Yunnan province would probably not have thrived in Hunan province, and vice versa. New strains would have to be bred, a methodical, time-intensive process still so new that only a few people in the world had the expertise to pull it off. We agreed the only way for the project to get off the ground in Cambodia would be to bring in four or five technicians, along with special fertilizer and botany equipment.

In collaboration with the Chinese, we contacted the appropriate technicians. Li Jing Yao, who had impressed me during my trip, was the world's foremost expert, and I insisted he be involved. I was funding the project out of pocket, so I could authorize travel expenses immediately. Everything began coming together quickly.

Of course, you can't plant rice without land. That problem proved easy enough to solve. During my political campaigns, I traveled from village to village to spread my message. I had many contacts from those days. Now I toured the countryside and spoke to the chief members of various villages. I explained what we were doing—to bring the new super rice to Cambodia, we needed several testbeds in different areas of the country. I asked the chiefs to find farmers who would be willing to donate one or two hectares of land. My team would do all the agricultural work. In the end, the farmers would keep the rice we produced.

By the time the technicians arrived from China, we had test sites in Kampong Speu, near Phnom Penh, in Takeo, and in Kampong Cham. In all, we had eight fields, which accounted for varying soils, rainfall, and climate. Due to the nature of hybridization and the growth cycle of rice, the entire process would take three years, at the end of which, if all went to plan, we would have abundant crops and irrefutable proof that the Chinese miracle could come to Cambodia.

•••

This period of optimism coincided with a very difficult stretch personally. Suganthini had been living in California for several months, and she was growing frustrated with my absence. I was deep in our project to bring rice to the people of Cambodia, and I didn't have time to nurture the relationship that had sustained me for so long. We spoke less and less, and finally Suganthini gave me an ultimatum. Return to California to live with her, or else she would seek a divorce. When she spoke these words over the phone, my heart sank. It was a devastating thing to hear from the woman with whom I shared so much. She was right—I had been neglectful as a husband and had not been a good or faithful partner to her. But I also knew that I couldn't abandon my project just as it was beginning.

In truth, I didn't fully believe that she would go through with the separation, although I never doubted that she was a woman of impressive will and resolve. I told her I couldn't join her in California, that I had unfinished business. It was the last time I spoke to her as my wife. She asked for a separation, and our long and fated love affair came to an ignoble end—one I hastened by my inattentiveness and ambition. I am incapable of expressing how much shame I still carry over this, my biggest failure. In the moment, however, I didn't have time to internalize how permanent our separation would be, or how much angst it would give me in the years to come. Things were moving too quickly to stop and think, so I put off the pain for some ugly day in the future.

And if I'm being truthful, there was another reason I could delay my conscience. Shortly after my separation to Suganthini, a new woman became a permanent part of my life. She was young and beautiful, and being with her gave me energy. We soon had a son, JC, and then she became pregnant again with a daughter, Jenny. I was bursting with pride and love at this surprise so late in life, and that joy helped me bury the festering pain of having allowed my first marriage to fail.

•••

The Chinese technicians began working at once, and I was busy helping them set up each of the sites—procuring equipment, signing papers, and making arrangements so they would be comfortable during their stay. In addition, I hired a group of Cambodian agricultural specialists. If the plan was going to work, it was imperative that the knowledge of the hybridization and agricultural techniques migrate to Cambodia, where that knowhow could germinate and spread.

The Chinese would become mentors to the Cambodian crew. Growing the seed was very complicated, requiring knowledge of specialized irrigation practices and soil chemistry. My role in the project, aside from funding, was to coordinate between the scientific teams; translate; and serve as an ambassador for our effort in the villages where we worked, in the Cambodian government, and in the international community.

It was also imperative from that start that I attempt to influence policy and drum up investment and support from the government or private industry. Going into the project, I knew that my $450,000 would not last the three years we would need to demonstrate viability. Though the Chinese were donating much of the seed stock and supporting the project logistically, I was paying all expenses. The project required significant travel and lodging for a small army. It would be a race against the clock to demonstrate positive results and win support from an outside sponsor.

With the effort underway, it was a joy seeing the Chinese technicians at work. They had deep knowledge of their field, and it became apparent that they thoroughly enjoyed sharing that knowledge. I remember the first time I saw one of the technicians speaking to a poor farmer who had donated land for our effort.

Asian culture is highly segmented, and people from different classes—people with different levels of education, for instance—don't always have a chance to intermingle. But the care the technician took explaining how to properly label fields, how to precisely measure and control water levels, and how to assess the health of fragile crops suggested a kind of universal connection born out of something deeper than class. The technician and the farmer, despite having completely different backgrounds, were both men of the soil whose livelihood was growing food for their brothers and sisters to eat. Out in the field, they treated each other as equals.

The project moved along promisingly for several months. I spent much of my time touring the sites and surrounding villages and solving logistical problems for the technicians. The rest of my time was spent lobbying for outside support. When our first crop came in, I sent samples of rice to every official and businessman in the country. Even Prince Sihanouk received a parcel of rice, along with an explanation of how it was grown and what the new strains could do for his country's economy. I got a kind note in reply. He thanked me for the gift, complimented the rice, and wished me luck on the endeavor. I was flattered by his kind words, but I began receiving similar replies from virtually everyone I contacted. Hun Sen, the prime minister, sent a long note as well.

All the feedback was encouraging, and everyone seemed eager to see the project succeed, but nobody seemed forthcoming with anything more than kind words. I pressed on, arranging tours of the rice paddies for VIPs. I invited the US ambassador to Cambodia, foreign agencies like USAID, and delegations from the UN, but nobody would agree to partner on the project.

Years later, after speaking about the promising technology with friends, I came to understand the problem. I was an advisor to the prime minister, a representative of the chamber of commerce, and a man who had twice run for political office and who, as far as anybody knew, might one day run again. Though my aim in bringing hybridized rice to the people of Cambodia was not political, but rather motivated by a combination of optimistic altruism and an interest in creating a stable business, I was also a connected man with specific political interests. In the minds of the people I approached, to back me would be to endorse my policies and political pursuits.

In a country where democracy was so young and the horrors of government-sponsored violence so fresh, it was always safer to avoid the appearance of backing anybody other than the ruling party. Even if I had understood this then, I still would have tried to bring hybridized rice to Cambodia. But I would have made every effort to distance myself from politics so people could judge the project on its own merits and not on my political leanings.

Toward the middle of our effort, my funds were so low I knew I couldn't continue. I made every attempt to attract a partner to take over and finish what, according to our early results, would have been proof of the miracle and promise of hybridized rice. But as I assessed the situation, I knew I had to pay the last of my debts with the money

I had left. I thanked the technicians with a heart full of gratitude and sent them home. The farmers who had lent us their land took the fields back, and I was proud that each of them came away from the project with a much fuller knowledge of the crop they had spent their entire lives growing. All the farmers we worked with professed to being happy about participating in the project, and they received a bounty of rice from our first harvests for their participation.

The failure was not one of science or vision, but of perception and execution. It is a lesson for anyone trying to do business in an emerging economy where suspicion abounds and politics sometimes obscures even the most promising opportunities.

With virtually no money left, I returned to my work at the chamber of commerce. But I soon found myself at odds with a prominent member of the chamber. The disagreement with this man over how he treated esteemed foreign investors became quite volatile, and under the guidance of a friend, I decided to return to California while things cooled off. I didn't understand how desperate things had become until I realized I couldn't afford the ticket.

It was a shock, as though I had fallen asleep rich only to wake up nearly destitute. The friend who encouraged me to return to California, a great man in Hun Sen's government named Phay Siphan, gave me money to buy a one-way ticket, returning a favor I had done for him a year or so earlier when he wanted to return to Cambodia from America to participate in the government. With a ticket in hand, I boarded a plane for LAX.

•••

The gravity of my situation again smacked me in the face. My only baggage was a small suitcase. I was carrying all the money I had left in the world, which amounted to less than one hundred dollars. I hailed a taxi outside LAX and took it to Long Beach. Imagine, then, that bright California sun beating down, the world awash in color and vitality, and me, a broken man with no connections and no one waiting to see me, sitting in the back of a taxi that I could barely afford, riding into an unknown future.

Suganthini wanted nothing to do with me, and it was just as well. I couldn't possibly face her in my state. My relationship with my grown children had suffered during my absence. They had nothing against me, and we were kind to each other whenever we spoke, but at that time I had done little to kindle the warmth that should exist in any happy family. In the back of the taxi, approaching Long Beach, I took stock of my long life. I was sixty-three years old. It was the saddest moment of my life.

Shrouded in self-pity, under the heavy weight of despair and failure, I went to the only place I could think of that might welcome an old man short on hope. During my time in California, I had become close with a Cambodian pastor named Luth Sin. His wife, Sok Kieng, was also a pastor, and during the day she ran a small salon. The taxi came to a stop on Anaheim Boulevard outside the salon. I paid the driver nearly all the money I had and dragged myself inside. A small bell above the door announced my presence, and Sok Kieng looked up, surprised to see me.

"Oh, Excellency," she said, using an honorific that, given the circumstances, I did not feel I deserved. "I thought you were in Cambodia." Once she had a chance to look at my face, she asked in a concerned, loving way, "What's happened?"

I took a seat in the salon, my suitcase on the floor between my legs, and told her it was a long story. I was very tired, and she told me to rest a while. It was evening by then, and in an hour she began closing her shop. She brought me to her house, where I greeted Luth Sin. Then, fighting tears, I told them my story. It seemed impossible that once more I had washed up in California without a penny to my name, just as I had in 1975. They listened with empathy. And then they prayed for me.

I would spend three and a half years in California, and aside from a brief trip back to Cambodia to visit my young son and my new wife, not one of those days was pleasant. With nowhere else to go, I moved in with Luth Sin and Sok Kieng. They were humble people and had very little room in their small home, but they gave with grace and selflessness. Perhaps because I was living with preachers, and perhaps because I had nowhere else to turn, I experienced a reawakening of my faith. I had converted to Christianity before my mother passed, at the height of my wealth in the 1980s. My elaborate baptism was, I thought, a kind of rebirth. But how can a man be born again if his life continues in much the way it always had? My faith helped me get over my gambling, but I cannot claim to have been devout in that period.

Now, with nothing, and with only a few acquaintances to help me, I turned to God. I acquired an old bible, which became one of my only possessions, and I read it from cover to cover. I attended several services a week, always trying to humble myself without feeling pity or regret. When I did pray for myself—and I tried to do so infrequently—I did not pray for money or for improved circumstances. I asked God for something far more precious. I prayed that He would deliver me contacts, people whom I could serve and who might, at some point down the road, be able to help me become useful again.

After a couple months, I knew I was imposing on my hosts. A woman from church offered to let me sleep on the covered porch outside her mobile home, and I took her up on her generosity. It was a small space, and in winter it was very cold. Water sometimes dripped from the roof and made the bed soggy. It was a far cry from my mansion in Vallejo, though I felt it was still more than I deserved. I shared dinners with the woman, and we attended services at a church where her son preached. It was a meager life, but I was grateful I was not entirely alone.

The contacts did not come at once. In fact, many contacts I believed I could rely on seemed to want nothing to do with me. One of the greatest heartaches I experienced in that period was seeing some of the same Cambodian immigrants I had helped back in the 1970s and '80s turn their backs on me. For some, I'm sure it was the memory of my gambling that kept them at bay. When I was gambling, I became more stringent about collecting rents, more demanding that the families leasing my shops pay on time. I had built my empire on trust and a fervent desire to help others, and in a few short years, in the grip of addiction, I undid a lot of the goodwill I had accumulated by becoming a cold businessman.

Still, it was disheartening to learn that even some people who had been close friends during the good times now wanted nothing to do with me. I was a fallen man living in disgrace, and they believed I was no longer of use. I felt discarded by my brothers and sisters. At times, sitting alone on the porch, I contemplated suicide. But then I turned to my bible, and I shook away such thoughts.

In 2005, while living on the porch, a *Los Angeles Times* reporter named Sam Quinones found me. He knew the story of the Cambodian donut entrepreneurs, and he had come looking for the man who helped a generation of immigrants find a foothold. He wrote a beautiful feature article about my life. The article was celebratory of my achievements, though ultimately it was tinged in sadness. It was called "From Sweet Success to Bitter Tears."

The saddest part of the story, to me, was that my young wife in Cambodia had given birth to my second child, a daughter, and I had not been able to witness it. When my daughter was born, she was very sick. I asked wealthy Cambodians who had made their money in the donut business for small loans of twenty dollars to send back to Cambodia, but they all turned me down. My wife was living at the top of a four-story apartment building, and the sun baked the roof during the day, making it too hot to stay inside. My young daughter, Jenny, was losing weight from vomiting, and my wife was suffering. I felt powerless.

I missed Cambodia, I missed my young family, and I cried frequently. At church, people encouraged me to go back as soon as I was able. The parishioners saw my agony, and they prayed for me. They also began giving me small sums of money—just a few dollars here and there. My wealthy contacts had nothing for me, but these poor people gave freely. I saved the money, and after several weeks I had enough for a plane ticket. The disagreement with the man from the Chamber of Commerce made returning to Cambodia difficult—though he never contacted me and did nothing to threatening me, I felt at the time that our political agreement might easily boil over into something more sinister. Such was the climate of a country crawling out of a generation of violence and despair. But I had to take the risk.

I boarded the plane feeling the full weight of my sixty-seven years on this planet. I was no longer a young man, and though I was healthy, I felt terrified that I would die before I had a chance to provide for my children or my country.

•••

Upon landing, I hired a *tuk-tuk* to carry me to my wife's apartment. She was living with her parents and our two small children in Phnom Penh. I was overjoyed to see my son and daughter, and over the next several days we fell into the joyful rhythms of family life. It was like a cool, refreshing drink of water after a walk through the desert. But the happiness would not last.

From the moment I walked in, my wife appeared fidgety and uncertain, and I sensed something was wrong. Sometimes the phone would ring, but nobody would be on the other end when I answered. The house seemed to swirl with some unspoken secret. Eventually, she came clean. In my absence, she had begun an affair with another man. After she told me, she suggested we get divorced. What could I say to that?

I had a job opportunity. Early in my career in the donut business, I had leased my shop in La Habra at a very low rate to a young man with no wife or children. He reinvested his income wisely, and soon, like many of the other donut entrepreneurs, he became wealthy. When he learned of my predicament, the man invited me to the coastal town of Kep on the Gulf of Thailand, a popular tourist destination. He owned a resort there, and he wanted to use my expertise in real estate to help him buy and sell land.

"Uncle," he said, using an honorific denoting respect, "you helped me when I was poor, and I want to repay the kindness." He told me he would pay me a few hundred dollars each month, and that he would give me a room and food. I was grateful and excited to become productive again, and I decided to move to the coast.

Now that I was reunited with my children, I knew I could not live without them. After much debate, my soon-to-be-ex-wife and I decided that I would take the children with me. She had looked after them for a long time in my absence, and though she loved our children very much, she needed a break. She certainly deserved one. We agreed to terms in a friendly way—I held no grudge, and I was grateful that she had been a good mother in my absence. When the divorce was finalized, my children and I took a bus from Phnom Penh to Kep, where a new future awaited.

But the future never arrives as expected. From the moment I landed, the man who had invited me treated me coldly. Instead of giving me my own room, as promised, he sent me to live with the maids and the workers. I didn't mind living that way, but he also refused to pay me. I couldn't understand this latest turn. I was surrounded by the most beautiful coastline in my country, and I looked out over the beautiful expanse of the Gulf of Thailand. My children, whom I was just getting to know, were so happy to be away from the city, and their smiles helped sustain me.

But I felt lower than ever, and I was running out of options. I told the man who invited me that he had broken his word, and I left the servants' quarters in hopes of salvaging some dignity. But the result was far from dignified: I was now homeless.

I appealed to a wealthy gentleman in town for help. In another life, we might have spoken as equals. But once you have fallen so low, it is a hard thing for a respectable person to see you as anything but a low man, and this gentleman could barely look at me. He had a second home in Kep, which he rarely used and was empty much of the year. Perhaps he would permit me to stay there until I figured out a more permanent living situation, I suggested. He told me the house was locked and he did not want me inside, but he would allow me to sleep on the porch with the children.

Now in my late sixties, I was back on a porch. We rolled out some mats to keep our bodies off the boards, where insects sometimes crawled up from the ground below. In nice weather, it wouldn't have been such a bad place to stay, except for the humiliation of living outside. But the wet season had arrived and rain clouds rolled on heavy winds from the Gulf of Thailand. The wind pushed the rain at an angle, smacking our faces and drenching our makeshift beds. For food, I spent a few pennies every day on noodles. I asked charitable people in town for boiling water and vegetables, and I made small pots of soup. I gave all the noodles to the children, who were growing and needed sustenance. I drank the broth and ate whatever portion of the vegetables were left over. Most of the time I stayed hungry.

It was a miserable way to live, but people have an odd way of growing accustomed to misery. That is how many millions survived the terrors of the Khmer Rouge without going insane, and it was how the three of us survived the anguish of living in abject poverty. My sole aim became the welfare of my children. It was imperative they receive an education, and when JC was old enough, I enrolled him in primary school. I borrowed a bike from a contact in town, and each day I peddled him to class early in the morning. I returned to pick him up at lunch time, when the school closed for a couple hours. I took him back in the afternoon, then picked him up in the evening. My eight daily trips added up to about forty kilometers—quite a distance for a man pushing seventy. My daughter, Jenny, began attending school not long after. In moments of hopelessness, the intelligence and bravery of children can change your attitude and lift you out of even the worst depressions.

•••

Helping those in need is an important responsibility in Cambodian culture. One day, a local policeman got word that I was living on the porch. He introduced himself and gave me a few dollars for dinner. The next day, he came back and asked if I would like to live in a small room in a local hotel. He said he would like to pay for the room and help feed me and my children. It was a generous offer, and for a few weeks we lived comfortably in the hotel, sharing many meals with the kind man.

Eventually, I began to feel bad. I knew that the policeman was not rich, and I felt guilty living off his kindness. It is a good thing to accept help when it is offered, but it is also good to observe the limits of that help. We moved back to the porch, but the man's generosity reminded me how much good there was in the world, and I believe it gave me a motivating jolt at just the right moment.

God also gave me hope. Every Sunday, I went to a local church gathering. The congregation had no money for a house of worship, so the preacher gave his sermon in the open air. Christians came from all around the region, and together we prayed and sang and gave thanks to God for all he did. I remember asking God to please give me just enough money to build a proper church, and I vowed that if I ever did have money again, I would use it to honor Him. I had been so foolish with my money before, so unwittingly selfish. Now I was humbled, and though I was suffering, I felt closer to the Divine.

When my son and daughter were finished with school each day, I quizzed them, and I found I enjoyed helping young people discover new corners of the world. This gave me an idea. I knew the deputy governor of Kep, an intelligent woman named Chamroeun Prum. She owned a very good seafood restaurant, which specialized in the excellent local crab that is one of Kep's regional staples. I asked Chamroeun Prum if I could use some space in her restaurant in the evening to teach English to local children for free. She thought it was a wonderful idea, and she even bought me a blackboard. The lessons were a big hit; I had twenty pupils in no time. More children heard about my class, and more parents, aware of the advantages speaking English could bring, encouraged their children to attend.

Before long, I was teaching a class of fifty, and finally one hundred students. It was like a miracle to see all their bright, smiling faces as they recited the alphabet and engaged in their first stumbling English conversations. It felt good to be giving back to the community in a positive way, and over the weeks I noticed a change in how others in the province spoke to me. I was no longer the fallen man. Now I was a local teacher, a good-hearted man who wanted to help others in spite of his own problems.

My new status brought new attention, and young businessmen familiar with the story of the donut king began asking my advice. A local *tuk-tuk* driver wanted to start a tourism business. His questions brought me back to my days giving tours around Phnom Penh, when I was a young man with a beautiful wife and my whole life in front of me. He was having trouble deciding if he should spend his savings on advertising. I listened to the pros and cons and told him, first and foremost, he needed to provide a good service. Without that, all the advertising money in the world would not help. If he had a good product, then I told him to take the risk with his savings. He had done the work to know that advertising was his best shot at getting noticed, and I felt strongly that taking the plunge was necessary to grow his business.

Perhaps in my present financial state I set a bad example of the perils of risk-taking, but I remained confident that a person who couldn't risk everything on an intelligent life decision would not advance. It is a truth I have never stopped believing. When the young man began buying advertising, his business picked up.

More young people came. Most of the time, their concerns had to do with having too little money. Kep is a poor place in a poor country, and the young entrepreneurs I spoke with worried that they wouldn't be able to get started with what little savings they had. I told them not to worry. They didn't have to wait to start their businesses. The most important component of success is a good idea, followed closely by resolve and hard work. If they could apply motivation, willpower, and drive to a promising idea, they could start a business. I told them my story, and I used my failure to show them that even with all the money in the world it is still possible to stumble.

•••

The deputy governor of Kep was pleased with the English lessons. She had her finger on the pulse of her province, and she knew I had been dispensing business advice to the town's would-be entrepreneurs. To encourage and formalize my efforts, she gave me $1,000 to set up a small consultancy offering free business guidance. It was more money than I had seen in a long time, and it was another kindness from a woman with great compassion and vision.

I continued dispensing advice, helping to launch the careers of youngsters with the same vision and hopes I had as a talented young man with nothing but ambition. The consultancy also attracted locals who needed help with small land deals, which can be very complex. I was well versed in the risks and possible rewards of buying and selling real estate, and I knew how to spot opportunities and negotiate good prices. The early deals

I helped shepherd were very small, but they afforded me tiny commissions that enabled me to provide real food for my children.

And then, as sometimes happens when you have lived a long life and tried, wherever you're able, to help others, a miracle occurred. Years earlier, when I had money and privilege and my future was bright in Cambodia, a young Chinese man had knocked on my door. Wang Yan Yu, the prominent and respected journalist turned businessman, needed help then. He saw extraordinary opportunity in the emerging market of Cambodia, and he believed the Chinese would begin investing massive sums. But his early attempts to broker land deals had ended in disappointment, and at that time, back in the mid-1990s, he was very poor.

I had seen immediately that he was a sharp man destined for big things. He was also a Christian, and perhaps in him I recognized some overt sign from God. I invited him to live with my family in Phnom Penh while he established himself, and when we parted ways as friends six years later, his career was on the rise.

Now, Mr. Wang called on me. After a long time stumbling alone in the cold, a visit from a familiar friend gave me new vigor. Mr. Wang was still living in Cambodia and working on various land deals with contacts back in China. He heard a rumor I was living on the coast and had come to find his old friend. I remember the feeling of brotherhood wash over me when I heard that. Then I remember feeling embarrassed at my state. I was poor, and though I was finding happiness in my work as a teacher and mentor to young people, I was no longer the respected businessman Mr. Wang had known in another life. That didn't seem to matter to him. We shook hands like old friends, and Mr. Wang told me how glad he was to see me.

We spent a long time that night catching up. I had not spoken Chinese in some time, and the language was like another old friend visiting from my past. I listened to the story of Mr. Wang's success, and I felt great pride in all his accomplishments. Then he listened to the tale of my failures and hardships. When that was out of the way, he asked for my help. His business contacts in China wanted to buy one thousand hectares of land in Cambodia. The deal would be incredibly complicated. In the United States, there is an elaborate system for purchasing land—real estate agents, lenders, escrow accounts, and insurers all work together to make buying and selling land a safe proposition for parties on both sides of a transaction.

In Cambodia, no such system exists. To buy land, it is imperative to establish a relationship with the seller, to investigate the legal status of the property, and to go very slowly to avoid mistakes and keep from being cheated. Mr. Wang had secured buyers, and now he needed help from somebody with intimate knowledge of Cambodia's business culture to close the deal. Most of all, he needed somebody he could trust. He asked if I would be willing to work with him. I didn't hesitate. The commission on a deal that large would be immense. But more important, I recognized in his miraculous and unexpected arrival a sign from above. Only a fool would turn it down.

The land in question was in Kampot, an urban coastal area not far from Kep. Over the next several months, Mr. Wang and I worked diligently to secure contracts. I assembled a team of trustworthy men to form a working group, and we began the arduous task of locking in rates with land owners, negotiating parallel contracts, and ensuring the deal went forward carefully. There were dozens of landowners, and any one of them could have disrupted our progress. These were stressful conditions to work under, but having gained and lost so much in life, I was not apprehensive. I knew that my fate was only partially in my hands, that all I could do was work diligently and honestly. For perhaps the first time in my life, I felt a kind of sublime joy in what I was doing.

I canvassed the countryside and spoke to landowners, as I had during the elections, and because we could give them fair rates, I spoke with great confidence that the deal I was offering was a good one. I also reserved a lot of time for my two children, who gave me a deep well of energy and love in my early seventies. And I prayed. I did not pray for success—that would take care of itself. I only prayed that whatever I was doing could help others in some way, which was the most important thing for a man in the final quarter of his life.

The deal went through. As soon as my commission arrived, I returned to Kep to fulfill a promise. I met with the preacher to whom I had listened so many times in my dark hours, and I asked him where he wanted his church. We chose an idyllic field set among rice paddies and water buffalo. I hired local workers to construct a road and then to build a large white building with a tile floor, one of the grandest structures in Kep. We had a ceremony to dedicate the church. The deputy governor came and gave a beautiful speech. I thanked her publicly for her grace and leadership, and I vowed to support her in all her endeavors to help her province's young people.

Over one hundred children were present at the ceremony. They ran through the beautiful, airy building in bare feet, laughing and playing tag. I recalled running with friends in my own childhood, and I thought of my mother, long dead now but surely looking down on the warm day. I thought of all the small choices and twists of fate that led me to that moment. Those children were just like me, all of them full of potential, all of them worthy of a chance. The church was their building—whether they came from Christian or Buddhist families, all were welcome. I hired an English teacher to give lessons. The children would come to this beautiful church on their bikes to receive a modern education. There is no progress without education. Cambodia is poor, but if money is invested in our most important resource, our children, then there is no limit to its potential.

After the ceremony, we had a banquet. I looked around at all the people who had made the trip. Many of them were important figures in the government whom I had known years earlier. Others were poor farmers who lived in nearby fields. There were men who had extraordinary wealth, almost all of whom had prospered from our struggle to gain MFN status and open Cambodia's economy. There were others who had been victimized by a brutal genocide and still had not recovered.

On that beautiful afternoon, in the shade of a canvas overhang that rolled gently in the wind, and amid the joy and cheer of a large feast, it was clear that all of us, no matter our backgrounds, felt hopeful. The world was brighter than it had been a day ago, and with God's mercy it would be brighter still tomorrow. Cambodia, a beautiful, tragic, resilient country, had endured so much. At long last, it was rising.

EPILOGUE

AN IMAGE FROM MY PAST COMES BACK TO ME NOW AND AGAIN, almost like a vision in reverse. I believe it is a glimpse at the most important moment of my life. The image is of me as a child getting off a bus in Battambang during my first year at boarding school. What is odd is that I see this scene so clearly, not from the perspective of the boy, who is me, but from the perspective of an onlooker. It is like having a front row seat to a life that is about to begin.

It may seem like a normal rite of passage—a boy going off to school—but I marvel at that boy. The probability of him ever making the journey was abysmally low. Children from my village didn't go to school beyond the mandatory elementary education. It was only through my mother's stubbornness in the face of financial reality, backed by her ingrained Chinese belief in the value of education, that I made that trip. It is because of the education I would get in Battambang, and later in Phnom Penh, that I had any say in my destiny.

While other countries in Asia have progressed mightily in the last few decades when it comes to educating their citizens, Cambodia is still mending wounds after a long stretch of turmoil. Literacy rates among children are rising, so the trends are moving in the right direction. Still, fewer than 40 percent of Cambodian children attend secondary school, according to UNICEF. Of those who are extraordinarily committed and graduate with high marks, only those from families with means can expect to attend university—a small fraction of the whole.

That is a travesty. Cambodia will never live up to its potential until a path to a university education is available to all. If the barriers to college were lowered, Cambodia could begin to transition away from the manufacturing economy it has built thanks to MFN status and toward an innovation economy, one in which citizens have a shot at working in offices and not garment factories, using their brain power and not their physical labor. This is the way economies progress. We have seen it most recently in other Asian countries such as Singapore, Hong Kong, Taiwan, and South Korea, the so-called Four Asian Tigers.

As I write this, Cambodia has enjoyed nearly a decade of 7 percent economic growth. It is primed to become a fifth Asian Tiger. But only if we invest in our potential— our human resources.

By God's grace, I am now rich again. It is almost comical how the pendulum of my life has swung to and fro. Working in collaboration with Mr. Wang, I have been fortunate to be involved in several land deals that have filled my accounts. My personal life has also been blessed. I am married to a beautiful woman and have children who fill me with love and energy. I feel so fortunate, and I feel called to give back.

My last dream is my most beautiful, I think. It is a direct extension of the image of that little boy and of the sacrifice and intelligence of my mother. I dream that the children of Cambodia will have their opportunity to thrive. To do it, they will require world-class education. That is why I am using the publication of my memoirs to pledge a seed endowment of $1 million to a new education foundation I am creating to provide scholarships to deserving Cambodian children. The foundation will target young children. By offering free college education on successfully completing primary and secondary school with high marks, we can begin to incentivize a new generation to hope for a better tomorrow.

It's a tomorrow I may not live to see. I am seventy-seven years old now. But I am nurtured by it just the same, strengthened by the beauty of this final dream of mine. I ask the readers of this book to make it their dream, as well, and to find ways to support the children of Cambodia and forge a future that is peaceful and prosperous.

CPSIA information can be obtained
at www.ICGtesting.com
Printed in the USA
LVOW13s1749150518
577262LV00013B/721/P

9 780999 432600